SEEING GOD

——— THROUGH ———

THE SCIENCE WINDOW

*Pondering the Wonders of Science,
Scripture, and Tradition in a Modern
Context for Deeper Faith*

JIM KRUPKA

WESTBOW
PRESS®
A DIVISION OF THOMAS NELSON
& ZONDERVAN

WestBow Press books may be ordered through booksellers or by contacting:

WestBow Press
A Division of Thomas Nelson & Zondervan
1663 Liberty Drive
Bloomington, IN 47403
www.westbowpress.com
844-714-3454

ISBN: 979-8-3850-2735-4 (sc)
ISBN: 979-8-3850-2736-1 (e)

Library of Congress Control Number: 2024912241

Print information available on the last page.

WestBow Press rev. date: 07/25/2024

CONTENTS

ACKNOWLEDGMENTS

The author wishes to recognize those who inspired this work and reviewed the manuscript for accuracy within their areas of expertise.

Ralph Treder, PhD. Retired Princeton and Bell Labs Physicist. Ralph's hours of conversations about the wonder of the Universe over lengthy walks and star-gazing chats added inspiration to this work.

Deacon Frank Olmsted: Theologian, educator, and clergyman who taught theology for 44 years at Catholic colleges and high schools. He served on the *Deacon Digest* editorial board and serves on the St. Meinrad Seminary Board of Overseers. He and his wife, Mary, were the first married couple to receive the St. Meinrad Seminary Distinguished Alumni Award.

Suzanne Krause Langford, PhD. Career educator and non-profit leader. She brought encouragement, contributing the perspective of social and human sciences as they intersect with faith.

Roger Clemmons, DVM, PhD, CVA, CVFT, DACVIM (Neurology/ Neurosurgery). Dr. Clemmons is a talented and inspirational leader in the science of Veterinary Neurology. He provided encouragement and insight blending science and faith.

Dr. Rosanne Krupka Peters, DVM, CVA, DACVIM (Neurology/ Neurosurgery). My oldest daughter, brilliant Veterinary Neurosurgeon and educator at the University of Illinois. Rose provided encouragement and technical review throughout this process.

Frances Kopp Krupka: My wife of over 50 years who has supported all my life's moves and been a beautiful partner throughout. I appreciate her patience with my development of this late-in-life career as a writer.

INTRODUCTION

The Universe is an amazing place. We look at the night sky and see what Abraham saw—a sky full of lights. Today we understand much more about those lights. With scientific knowledge, we see enormous galaxies full of stars—some with planets. We understand that the lights we see show us worlds as they were thousands and even billions of years ago.

Here on Earth, we know of the complexity of the human body and things around us that were not known just a hundred years ago. We know of tremendous forces within our world, like nuclear energy, far exceeding any earthly force known before. We know that our world is very old, in human terms at least. Far older than our great-grandparents ever imagined. From some of the same observations, we know that much of the science we inherited from our ancestors was right and accurate. We know much more about things like gravity and chemistry, but the basics still hold. We also see that the basic laws describing forces and how things move are as true now as ever.

We have matters of faith—our beliefs. Faith has been an important part of human life for thousands of years. Our beliefs drive how we think about ourselves and the world around us. Faith gives us hope that drives us to adopt a way of life that is loving and sacrificial.

Many faith traditions draw from experiences that were recorded in writing, largely several thousand years ago. Faith tells us that a divine God guided the hands of the writers, but the manuscripts were written by humans living at a certain time in history. The images they provided were drawn from what they saw and what their contemporaries knew at the time. Applying those writings to what we know today generally delivers the same moral lesson but different details.

Humans are learning creatures. Many of the features of life described in Christian New Testament Scripture were unheard of when the first book of the Bible, Genesis, was written. Similarly, in the 2,000 years since the Christian texts were written, learning continued. Much of this learning has come through science. Sciences like anthropology, which looks at historical human life, or cosmology, which looks at the origin and makeup of the Universe, give us windows into who and what we are. Some of that understanding leads us to ponder some of the "why" we are.

Science and faith go together. Faith describes God's goodness as the source of all we have. Among the things God has given us is knowledge via science. We can see that continue as our window into the wonder of Creation grows all the time.

At this point in history, we have a choice. Some look to science as the ultimate measure of truth. Observations can be tested through the scientific method and be shown to be true or false. Others put absolute trust in faith, especially as recorded in the Bible, as the ultimate test of truth on everything. Most people draw from both.

Mysteries of faith and science can be equally challenging. Our human minds and will to learn take us deep, but some things remain beyond absolute proof and understanding. For many of us, we cannot raise anything that looks like a doubt in our faith communities. That's too bad because that is how we learn.

This book is written for ordinary people who are working hard to understand life and seek truth. A point of this book is that it is okay to wonder. Wondering in a search for truth is not lazy doubt. Seeking truth is a moral must, necessary to nurture an informed conscience to guide us to God.

The order of this book aims to show how faith and science illuminate each other. Date references use the modern labels and abbreviations of "Before Common Era" or "B.C.E." for times counted backward from the modern Western calendar years. Dates aligned with our current calendar are "Common Era" or "C.E." Before these modern labels took hold, the same dates were known as "Before Christ" or "B.C." and "Anno Domini" or "A.D." A.D. is the Latin translation of "Year of Our Lord." The Western World generally aligns its numbering of years to the coming of Christ. A monk named Dionysius (500 C.E.+/-) invented the concept of Anno Domini. Dionysius did not know the exact year of Jesus' birth; however, he was close. Theologians believe the actual birth of Jesus was 4 to 6 years B.C.E.

What we see in science increasingly shows us how incredible God's work in Creation is. The new discoveries do not undercut faith. For someone who really considers what we learn from science, faith grows. I begin with a look at the creation of the Universe, considering Scripture and science. The two descriptions are more alike than many think. Second, we look at the creation of humanity, considering Scripture and the science of evolution. The two descriptions are also more alike than many admit. Third, the book addresses several topics describing scientific discoveries in the last century. Among the discoveries is the understanding of the basic composition of the stuff we are made of—atomic structure. Einstein's findings on the connection of mass and energy, as well as the variability of time and space, are also considered.

Following the mysteries of science, several mysteries of faith in a practical sense are discussed. This includes pondering what God is really like or where and what is heaven. The last section of the book looks at human experiences that lead us to God. Archeological evidence tells us that ancient cultures had an awareness of God that resembles what a believer sees today. God worked within them. They got there without any formal exposure to the Gospel.

On all these big questions, the book presents evidence without conclusions. In the end, the reader must decide. To believe or not to believe. That is a question for eternity.

PART ONE

EARTH, UNIVERSE, AND HUMANITY

I-1: Biblical Window to God: It's More than the Literal Words.

Scriptures begin with a detailed description of Creation. The literal description of the creation event says it happened in six days, followed by a day of rest. The words describe a completed world by the end of those six days. The words describe the Earth and the visible surroundings. There was the Earth, the oceans, the sky, and lights in the sky. There was a landmass separated from the oceans and life growing upon it.

The Christian Church into the 1600s did not vary significantly from that description. The observation window did not reveal much beyond. The secrets of space and the composition of matter and human beings remained mysteries. Under the twin drivers of practicality and faith, there was no need to look deeper. Since then, scientific observations have provided much more detail of what exactly the lights in the sky are or what sub-microscopic pieces make up matter within and around us.

People did ponder questions like how old the Earth is and how, exactly, God did all of this. Before the 17th century, the Catholic Church was the authority on the details. The Church drew from Old Testament history to describe the physical makeup of the Earth. It drew from those same Scriptures to determine the age of the Earth. In the 1600s, churchmen determined the Earth to be around 6,000 years old. Soon after, observations of the Earth itself led to a much more complex and long-term picture.

How do we reconcile this difference between the pre-1600 description of the Earth and discoveries through actual observation since? A good place to start is a look at what many people of science and faith have in common. For most, there is respect for Scripture as an inspired window leading to God. Second, the wonder of Creation far exceeds the product of chance. Third, this all had to start somehow. There had to be some initiating force. Fourth, we continue to gain more knowledge from faith and science about the Universe we live in. We cannot ignore what we see. To do so would be to do injustice to the wonder of God.

The Catholic Catechism addresses this tension with words encouraging us to look into the science window. We read, "The question about the origins of the world and of man has been the object of many scientific studies which have splendidly enriched our knowledge of the age and dimensions of the cosmos." (CCC283) These discoveries invite us to "greater admiration of the greatness of the Creator." Theologian Raymond Brown points out that "Christianity has been at its best" when "it has been able to digest and profit from every new major body of knowledge."

The Introduction to the New American Bible discusses how we should interpret the creation story in Genesis. The introduction reminds us that the stories are neither history nor myth. They convey truth. But to call it history is misleading. In that introduction, we are reminded that "Ancient Near Eastern thinkers did not have our methods of exploring serious questions. Instead, they used narratives for issues that we would call philosophical and theological. They added and subtracted narrative details and varied the plot as they sought meaning in the ancient stories." Raymond Brown affirms the Bible as the "Word of God." But he points out that because humans captured the word, there were human limitations on what those writers could absorb. Think about how fruitless it would have been for God to drop the full substance of astrophysics into the minds of the pre-2000 B.C.E. writer. The intent of Divine revelation was to teach about God and morality, not details of biology or physics.

To get the most out of the Bible, we must go beyond the "literal" to get the whole substance and revelation from Scripture. We must use all we have, including scientific, literary, and historical methods, to understand the full meaning. As these sciences advance, we learn about the conditions under which the Scripture writers were living. They had to put revelation in terms that would focus the reader of their time on understanding God, not the details of science. Historical analysis lets us consider what they knew about the world, humanity, and the Universe. We must consider how they used stories and images to convey divine revelation. Storytelling has been a basic part of passing knowledge from one generation to the next in most, if not all, cultures. Think about how most preachers today include some kind of story in their sermons to grab the attention of their flock.

The writers of Genesis were not around when the Earth was formed. The approximate intersection between stories crafted to explain existence without direct observation and later stories based on direct observation is the Exodus. Nobody was around to record the details of the Garden of Eden or the Great Flood. But by the time of Exodus, history was being recorded from direct observation. At that time, the Jewish people had a relationship with God but had no direct witness to how their existence and this relationship with the Divine came to be. They had to draw from inspiration and what they saw around them. They also drew from common accounts of existence from other sources, including pre-existing myths. The story of Noah and the Great Flood is similar to a Mesopotamian story of a great flood as recorded in their Gilgamesh Epic.[1]

As writers filled the gap from the unseen beginning of time to the Exodus, they were inspired and pondered the world's origin. Above all, they were teaching of the universal sovereignty of God. Part of that lesson was to establish God as the absolute creator. He is the source of the world and humanity.

Of particular interest to the first Scripture writers was conveying God's special relationship as the source of the Hebrew nation and people.[2] As we read the Scripture, we need to understand that the Hebrew nation was their audience. To make their points about God, they had to use images that were present among the people of the time. Writing is a literary art that conveys images, ideas, and emotions through words. The words need to connect with the reader or hearer. This sets up meaningful parameters to help us fully understand the Bible.

We cannot take words literally that were written to connect to a long-ago audience. The words were written in a way that they could get the message to the target audience who lived at a point in human history far different from ours. They had a certain context that, in some ways, was just like ours but, in some ways, vastly different. Context, like the love between a man and woman in marriage, fits today just like it did 6,000 years ago. The context of the immensity of the Universe is vastly different now than then. The Introduction to the New American Bible cautions that "the truths themselves must therefore be clearly distinguished from their literary garb." Literary garb has a purpose. The literal words allow the reader to understand something beyond their immediate observation. But the garb appropriate to a point today may be quite different from the garb to convey the same point 6,000 years ago.

The purpose of this book is to look into the science window to more fully see the greatness of God. As we do this, there will be a combination of historical and literary elements to connect findings of faith and science. The words herein are part of a current-day literary "garb" to see the wonder of God. We are after the same result as the Biblical authors of old.

I-2: What Picture of the Universe Can We Draw from Genesis?

In Genesis, the Earth starts as a vast wasteland without form as darkness covered the "abyss." Winds swept over the ocean. The waters of the ocean surrounded it all as God created a dome with water below and above.[3] A common image developed from these words shows the Earth supported by pillars above the ocean. Picture the wasteland as a barren, flat desert. Scripture describes the creation of a "dome" to separate the waters above and below. This dome was the sky.[4] Openings in the dome allowed rain to fall. Lights were added to the sky—the stars of night. The desert was drawn up into a landmass to support life of all kinds. Below the depths was Sheol, the home of the dead.[5]

At the time of the writing of the beginning of the Bible, this was the world they observed. There were no direct witnesses to the actual creation event. The creation narrative establishes God as the creator. That is accurate and remains absolute through our observations today. But the details of what the Earth and Universe look like, are far different today. The difference does not diminish God's role. On the contrary, the immensity of what we know today is immensely more awesome than the picture held by the pre-Christian Hebrews. We now can start to understand God, Christ, as king of the Universe in a much deeper way than our predecessors.

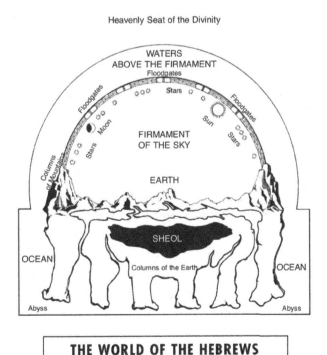

THE WORLD OF THE HEBREWS

Image Source: New American Bible presented as part of Genesis Chapter 1.

Then, as now, science is based on observation. The words of Genesis 1 describe what people of pre-2000 B.C.E. saw out their science window.

I-3: How Old Is the Earth?

How long has humanity been around? In 1650, Irish Anglican Bishop James Ussher published a detailed history of the world in a work called *The Annals.*[6] It was over 2,000 pages long. The date that made Ussher famous appears in the first paragraph of the first page of *The Annals.* Ussher wrote: "In the beginning, God created heaven and earth, which beginning of time, according to this chronology, occurred at the beginning of the night which preceded the 23rd of October in the year 710 of the Julian period." Ussher computes the date in "Christian" time to be 4004 B.C.E.[7]

For centuries, Christians assumed a date similar to Ussher's based on Biblical events. Taking events in the Bible literally, we can conclude that Creation occurred less than 5,000 years before the birth of Christ. Others near and around Ussher's time came up with a similar number. We find in Shakespeare's work, *As You Like It,* the character Rosalind says, "The poor world is almost six thousand years old." Martin Luther professed the date of creation to be about 4000 B.C.E. Even scientists arrived at the same date. Astronomer and mathematician Johannes Kepler, in the early 1600s, concluded that creation happened in 4997 B.C.E.

Ussher, Kepler, and other contemporaries drew literally from Scripture to arrive at the age of the Earth. The Word of God in Holy Scripture gave us the details. "In the beginning, when God created the heavens and the earth—and the earth was without form or shape, with darkness over the abyss and a mighty wind sweeping over the waters—Then God said: Let there be light, and there was light." (Genesis 1:1–3). The account continues. There was formation of the oceans and land. Then came vegetation followed by "animals of all kinds." All of this took five of the six "working" days of creation. On day six, the big event happens. Scripture says in Genesis 1:27, "God created mankind in his image; in the image of God he created them; male and female he created them." Humanity is the last addition to the master plan of creation. As the sixth day ended, God proclaimed that all was "good" and rested on day seven. This is the engineer's story of creation. All happens step by step in a logical way without much emotion.

Moving from the biblical creation account through Scripture builds the case for a world that is 6,000 years old. Genesis 1 says that the Earth was created on the first day of creation (Genesis 1:1–5). From there, we can begin to calculate the age of the Earth. The age of the Earth can be estimated by taking the genealogies from Adam to Abraham in Genesis 5 and 11, then adding the time from Abraham to today.

The Bible says that Adam was created on day six, so there were only five days before him in all of creation. In the context of this calculation, those five days are beyond roundoff error. Taking the genealogies in the Bible from Adam to Abraham, that history encompassed about 2,000 years. We read that in Genesis 5 and 11. The life of Abraham was late enough in world history to be tangibly part of Hebrew history credibly recorded. As such, Christian and secular scholars generally agree that Abraham lived about 2,000 years B.C.E. With Adam present only six days into the created world, the Earth was about 2,000 years old at Abraham's time. From the time of Abraham, it took about 2,000 years to get to the birth of Christ. Scripture is a source for that number.[8]

The sum of 2,000 years to get from the time of Christ to today is solid. Adding these three 2,000-year periods together makes the Earth 6,000 years old. This fact is literally recorded in Scripture. Who can speak against that?

> Year Zero: Creation
> Year 2000: Abraham as the Father of God's people.
> Year 4000: Christ is born.
> Year 6000: The world of today, the 21st century.

In the 17th century, the "when" of creation was accepted as common knowledge. Note that all the sources were European. A unifying factor in this Europe-centered world was the Church. Unity came via beliefs and the common language of Latin.

That was right and proper since Europe was the center of thinking, knowledge, and civilization. The "New World" to the west was just beginning to develop European-style civilization. The island civilizations of the Pacific were largely unknown. The ancient civilizations of China and the East were just being discovered.

The world beyond Europe remained little understood into the 18th century. Claudius Ptolemy worked in Alexandria in the early and mid-2nd century C.E. He provided a map that reveals what people of his era knew about the extent of the Earth. Unlike some who imagined a flat Earth, Ptolemy saw the world as a sphere. This map came from his popular book "Geographia." Ptolemy accounted for space in new ways based on mathematical calculations, using coordinates for lands giving a comprehensive image of the size of the Earth. His map influenced medieval mapmakers. It was hidden until it was rediscovered during the Renaissance. In his depiction of the Earth, Ptolemy showed the inhabited area as a small part of the world. His map showed the inhabited Earth limited to an area from the tropical south extending north to about the Arctic Circle. The east-to-west extent went from Malaya west to the Atlantic. Ptolemy's description of geography endured for a very long time. Editions of Ptolemy's work were published in Italy in 1477, over 1,000 years after his death. It is evident that the understanding of the geography of the Earth did not advance much during all of that time.[9]

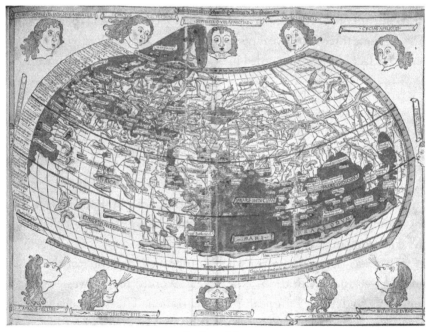

Ptolemy Map

Until the mid-1800s, the age of the Earth was widely accepted as about 6,000 years. This rested solidly on Biblical events. But science was bringing more information to the subject. In the mid-nineteenth century, calculations ranged from 5,400 to almost 9,000 years.[10] The expansion of the range of ages came as evidence grew from geologic evidence, like fossils and stratification of deposits, that challenged the "one shot" creation theory. Scientists approached the subject with reverence and respect for the Bible. The idea that the Bible was never meant to be a science or literal history book was just starting to develop.

Into the 18th century, studies of the layering of rocks near the surface of the Earth, called strata, led scientists to observe that Earth may have been through many changes over time. These layers often contained fossils of life that were not present at the time of observation, hinting at early life far distant in time from the present.[11] Nicolas Steno, in the 17th century, was one of the first. The 17th-century naturalist Steno discovered the connection between fossil remains and strata. He proposed several geologic concepts that are common knowledge today. His observations led him to formulate important stratigraphic concepts like the "law of superposition" and the "principle of original horizontality." The basics of geology as the mirror of time are rooted in these laws. As new source material for rock formations is deposited at a site, younger layers stack atop older layers.

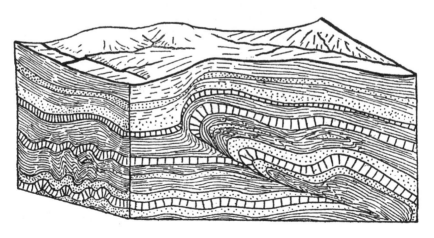

Rock strata below the surface of the Earth

Late in the eighteenth century, William Smith could see that two rock layers at widely differing locations contained similar fossils. He proposed that the layers were the same age. Smith's nephew, John Phillips, continued the work and calculated the Earth to be about 96 million years old.[12] The work of Smith and Phillips did not receive broad attention.

By the mid-19th century, geologic evidence supporting that the Earth was far older than 6,000 years grew to the point that a challenge to the literal biblical age could be made. In 1862, Lord Kelvin made a numerical calculation of Earth's age. Kelvin used information from physical sources outside the Bible.[13]

Kelvin knew that Earth's temperature increased one degree Fahrenheit for every fifty feet of depth below the Earth's surface. Kelvin estimated that the Earth began as molten rock. Then he calculated how long it took to cool the planet to the observed surface temperature gradient. He said it would take one hundred million years to reach one degree every fifty feet. This delivered a huge challenge to the accepted age of 6,000 years, which invigorated biblical literalists. Kelvin's estimate also was attacked by scientists, like Darwin, who saw evidence for the Earth being far older than Kelvin's estimate.

Layers of the Earth from the "cool" surface to "hot" core.

Today, there is little doubt that the Earth is very old—in the billions of years. Sources generally present an age for the Earth of four and a half billion years within a Universe that is nearly fourteen billion years old.[14]

Scientists today center on 13.7 billion years as the age of the Universe. They arrive at that conclusion by looking for the oldest stars. They also measure the rate of expansion of the Universe from the birth event that we call the Big Bang. The measurements made by NASA have shown that the Universe is 13.7 billion years old, plus or minus about 130,000 years.[15]

As we do this hunt for answers to questions like how old the Earth is, we look to scientists with special skills in fields like cosmology to process what humankind observes with our advanced tools, like space-based telescopes. Scientists can take detailed observations from today's tools combined with accumulated science to make an estimate of the age of the Universe. In the case of the recent age of Universe calculations, scientists used Einstein's Theory of General Relativity to 'run the clock backward to time zero—the Big Bang birthday of the Universe. The interval between then and now is calculated to be 13.7 billion years.

This is not a physics book, so I will not go much deeper into exactly how all these discoveries came about. What I hope this bit about the age of the Universe will do is motivate you to look into the science window and see what those who have the skill to use the data find. I assure you, it is very interesting. Likewise, I am certain there are many amazing discoveries yet to come.

I-4: How Was the Earth Formed?

The discussion so far has been on the age of the Earth. Related to that question is how did it all happen? Did God just wish it, and in an instant, it all happened? Findings about the age of the Earth and indications of some sequence in creation, like the rock strata, bring awareness that maybe the Earth and all its creatures were not delivered as a finished product in one wink of God's eye.

Wrapped up in the first chapter of Genesis, we have the complete steps of creation from nothing to the existence of human beings as we know humanity today. The entire process took six days. Humans were created on the spot in final form and presented with a finished, all-inclusive Earth to enjoy. The sequence of creation was:

Day One: Heaven and Earth, Energy of the wind. Light. Differentiation of night and day.

Day Two: Sky above the ocean.

Day Three: Dryland raised above the oceans, Vegetation in the form of plants and trees.

Day Four: Sun and moon and stars. Day and night.

Day Five: Crawling creatures, birds, fish, and other animal life (living creatures).

Day Six: Animals of all kinds, tame and wild. Seed-bearing plants. Human beings with a commission to have dominion over creation.

Day Seven: God rejoiced in his creation and rested.

Adam and Eve in the Garden of Eden

St. Augustine, late in the fourth century, commented on creation as recorded in Genesis. He maintains that the answer is clear in Scripture. From the first instant of time, God created the world out of nothing. However, Augustine did ponder the sequence of creation in scripture. He wondered about how the creation of light on the first day (Let there be light) coincided with the creation of the Sun, the moon, and the stars on the fourth day. Augustine dealt with this paradox by proposing that God "made all things at once."[16] Augustine's thinking led to the extreme "all in an instant" description of Creation.

Discoveries about the age of the Earth and its progressive development do not support the concept of Creation as a finished product in one instant. So, does this fly in the face of God as the Creator and the majesty of his work? Not so. Science and religion are much closer to each other than many think when it comes to the creation of the Universe. Sir Isaac Newton, the 17th-century mathematician who is the source of understanding of the laws of gravity and physical motion, believed that our solar system did not "arise out of chaos by the mere laws of nature."[17] He said the Universe was "created by God at first and conserved by him to this day in the same state and condition."[18] His science window supported God as an Almighty creator. Newton saw a more impressive and ordered creation than Augustine's "one and done" model. From Newton's time, scientific discoveries advanced at a rapid pace. But each discovery brought a grander picture of the created Universe.

In the 19th and 20th Centuries, scientists detected other details of the Universe occurring over billions of years extending far beyond the Earth. The great astrophysicist Stephen Hawking provides an excellent summary of the physical creation in his book *The Grand Design.*[19] The title of Hawking's book is revealing. Even though he was not able to come to terms with the existence of God, he acknowledged that the chance that random events would lead to the Universe and Earthly life as we know it is extremely small. He made a case for intelligent design.

The Big Bang

Today there is widespread acceptance of a grand start to the Universe beginning with an amazing explosion commonly referred to as the Big Bang. Just as the theme song to the TV show *Big Bang Theory* says, it all started with the substance of the Universe consolidated in a tiny, hot, dense state. This tiny ball was small. All of the energy of the Universe we see was squeezed into a space the size smaller than a grain of sand.[20] This may have been the remainder of a previous universe that collapsed upon itself or the first seed of an all-new universe.[21] Either way, the question remains, how did the "seed" get there in the first place? That was a key part of Theologian, Thomas Aquinas' argument in favor of the existence of God. Something had to pre-exist in the Universe to give the substance and push for the Big Bang.

From what we know now, the first moments of the Universe were incredible. In a minuscule fraction of a second, the Universe expanded to the size of galaxies. This micro-micro second period of our Universe is called "inflation." The whole lot of the Universe expanded like a rapidly inflating balloon. There really is no center or "zero point" for the Universe. As inflation progressed, bits that would become individual galaxies moved away from each other like points on the skin of a balloon.

*Expanding Universe: Galaxies move apart like the
points on the surface of a balloon or bubble.*

In the first second of time, space and the laws of physics very quickly solidified. From there, order started to emerge out of the chaos. First to take shape were subatomic particles. Then bigger particles like protons and neutrons. Technically, protons and electrons formed directly from the energy available in the ultra-hot Big Bang, and then neutrons, via proton-electron collisions, formed. The first nuclei were the protons. The first atoms were pure hydrogen. Fusion of hydrogen nuclei became the basis for helium once neutrons were formed. About three minutes later, the Universe had cooled to 1 billion °C. This allowed protons and neutrons to come together through fusion and form nuclei, the charged cores of atoms. The most common product of fusion is the element helium. The center nucleus of helium contains two protons and two neutrons fused together. The source of matter for this fusion process is the hydrogen nucleus. The fusion of hydrogen to form helium is the ongoing heat engine within our Sun.

Helium nucleus: Two protons, two neutrons.

But after 20 minutes, the Universe was no longer hot enough for fusion. What was left was a hot, cloudy soup of electrons and hydrogen and helium nuclei. This stage lasted for about 380,000 years. Eventually, the cosmos cooled enough for electrons to pair up with nuclei and make the first atoms. It then took hundreds of millions of years for the first stars to form and light up the darkness and even longer for the Universe to start to resemble what we see today. That is why a significant difference exists between the scientific age of the Universe, generally thought of as 13.7 billion years, and the age of the Earth, widely believed to be 4.5 billion years.[22]

The Church has no official position on the age of the Earth. The Catechism of the Catholic Church says that the findings of modern science have splendidly enriched our knowledge of the age and dimensions of the cosmos, the development of life forms, and the appearance of man. These discoveries invite us to even greater admiration for the greatness of the Creator, prompting us to give him thanks for all his works and for the understanding and wisdom he gives to scholars and researchers. (CCC283)[23]

I-5: Creation of the Stuff of Matter: Chemical Elements

The Creation sequence during the initial moments of the Universe set in motion the conditions for the matter that we call elements to take shape. In our high school chemistry classes, we learned about the Periodic Table of elements and the vast diversity of natural elements. Elements range from light-weight hydrogen to heavy uranium.

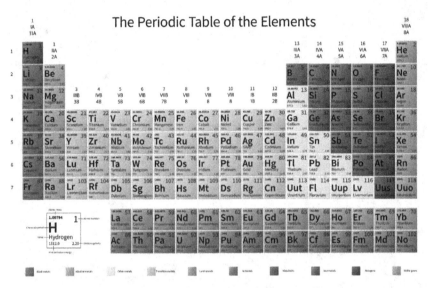

Periodic Table of Chemical Elements.

The sequence began with the formation of the first elements. During the first 200 seconds of the Universe, the primary elements of the Universe, the light elements of hydrogen, helium, and lithium, were "synthesized" under the intense heat and subsequent cooling. This was nuclear fusion to the extreme. Still to be formed were the heavier elements that are necessary for life, carbon, and oxygen.

Fusion of Hydrogen Nuclei to form Helium.

As the grand design continued, over four billion years passed before conditions were right for collections of heavy atoms to be attracted to each other to form bodies like our Earth. Scientists say the path to the Earth's formation was at least a two-step. Further nuclear fusion beyond hydrogen to helium was needed to progress and fuse heavier elements into even heavier elements. In the grand Universe, this happens as a star matures. The hydrogen-to-helium fusion furnace shuts down as the star's fusion furnace runs out of fuel. This results in matter being pulled back into a tiny dense ball under intense heat and pressure. This pressure and heat-driven furnace jams lighter elements together to fuse those light elements into heavy elements. At that point the dying star is about at its end. Ultimately, that dense, heavy, and dying star explodes, pitching light and heavy elements into space. When a large amount of that debris from the star's explosion ends up in a particular area of space, they are pulled together by gravitational attraction. That gravitational attraction brings those heavy elements to amass into bodies that become new stars and planets. In our case, such a collection became Earth.

So, to get to the Earth that we know today, with its rich assortment of life-supporting elements, we needed several things. Billions of years beyond the Universe-forming Big Bang passed. Then, we needed an Earth-specific big bang. The unique big bang that gave the elemental seeds for the Earth was the destruction of that dense, ancient star. Prior to that Earth-specific big bang, we required the fusion of the light elements into heavier ones within that dying star. Then, we required the accumulation of heavy elements in the ultra-dense star to disperse via an explosion, sending the full array of light to heavy elements into space. With the seeds of a planet cast into space, the formation of a planet requires that there be enough matter in a portion of space to allow the accumulation of that matter into a gravitationally formed sphere. That was the case as a collection of matter coalesced into a sphere to become our planet Earth.

But much more was necessary to have that sphere in a position to support life. The new planet had to be just the right distance from the sun to provide the conditions for life. In our case, the sphere formed at a perfect distance from the Sun. Further, the distance had to be just right to balance the gravitational attraction between Earth and the Sun to keep our Earth in this life-sustaining place rather than drifting off into frigid space or stellar incineration. That, folks, is a pretty grand design, far more likely than pure chance.

Think of the similarities to Genesis. In the beginning, there is darkness. Then there is a sudden appearance of the physical components of the Universe. Our Sun, other stars, moons, and planets appear. We have light. Chemical elements are built from the basic stuff of matter. The chemical stuff combines to form heavier elements, especially carbon, to be the building blocks of life. The basic path is the same. The creation chapter in Genesis highlights the goodness of creation and the Divine desire that human beings share in that goodness. In the Bible, God brings an orderly Universe out of primordial chaos merely by uttering a word. In the Big Bang, the same orderly Universe comes in an infinitely small instant.

As we apply our human hearts and minds to understanding how we came to be, humans throughout history have been led to believe in the existence of God. When we try to comprehend things like the infinite power of God or eternal existence, understanding creation as expansive beyond our imagination or time horizons into the billions of years, we are drawn to believe in the unseen God. The science window gives us a look at the power of God that validates the moral lessons of the Bible. God is all-powerful. God exists without beginning or end. God is the only source imaginable to provide the initial push for the wonder that science shows us.

PART TWO

THE ORIGIN OF LIFE

Paradise Complete: Man and Woman in the Garden of Eden

The Garden of Eden by Jan Brueghel de Oude & Peter Paul Rubens. Early 17ᵗʰ century CE. (The Royal Picture Gallery Mauritshuis, The Hague, Netherlands)[24]

II-1: The Origin of Human Beings.

The billions of years leading to the physical Earth we know today describe an evolving planet and Universe. From the hot, dense accumulation of matter in a tiny space 13.7 billion years ago came the Big Bang and rapid expansion of the Universe. Matter cooled to allow the formation of elements that were attracted to each other to form stars and planets. Around 4.5 billion years ago, the Earth coalesced and cooled to occupy a spot located at the perfect distance from a star, our Sun, to support life. This could be described as a process of physical evolution leading to the perfect circumstances that allowed life to form. Within those perfect circumstances, one special life form capable of a spiritual relationship with God evolved, humanity.

The same authors who recorded that the creation of a fully finished Earth occurred in six days speak of a fully developed human being brought onto that Earth on day six. In the first chapter of Genesis, human beings are at the tail end of the creation story. Understanding that the Earth is billions of years old rather than just 6,000 years raises the challenge of when, in that time period, humans as we know them come to be. Perhaps it was only 6,000 years ago. God, in his wisdom, could have determined that the time was right for this special creature to occupy the Earth.

As stated earlier about the use of the Bible to answer physical questions, we remember that the Church says, "The question about the origins of the world and of man has been the object of many scientific studies which have splendidly enriched our knowledge of the age and dimensions of the cosmos." (CCC283). When we look at these discoveries, we get a greater admiration for the greatness of the Creator. Taking an approach like we do to determine the age of the Earth; we look in the science window to see what we can find about human existence on the planet. Do we see evidence of humans being on this planet for more than 6,000 years? Science gives a window into the answer.

This order could easily allow for billions of years of Earth's history to pass before humans appeared. In Genesis One, step by step, the Earth, sky, and stars are formed out of nothing. Then plants and animals. Finally, humans. While the literal words of the Bible say the creation of the Earth happened in six days, we know from physical evidence that the creation of the Earth took billions of years. With God operating outside any limit or definition of time, the Bible and science are compatible. Six days for God are not the same as six rotations of the planet Earth that we call days.

The time and sequence of creation can be appreciated more from the second chapter of Genesis. This second Biblical account of creation has human beings at the center of the story. In the second chapter of Genesis, human beings are the focus around which the rest of creation happens. In Genesis 2:4–7, we read,

> This is the story of the heavens and the earth at their creation. When the LORD God made the earth and the heavens—there was no field shrub on earth and no grass of the field had sprouted, for the LORD God had sent no rain upon the earth and there was no man to till the ground, but a stream was welling up out of the earth and watering all the surface of the ground—then the LORD God formed the man out of the dust of the ground and blew into his nostrils the breath of life, and the man became a living being

Note that "days" or a timetable are unimportant in this account. There is also no attempt to detail all the steps in the creation process. What is important is that God made it all. He made Heaven and Earth and then formed man to dwell within them. With the arrival of the first human, God brought the trees, plants, and all that was good. In Genesis 2:8–9, we hear how paradise was built around that human being.

> The LORD God planted a garden in Eden, in the east, and placed there the man whom he had formed. Out of the ground the LORD God made grow every tree that was delightful to look at and good for food, with the tree of life in the middle of the garden and the tree of the knowledge of good and evil.

The Intersection of the Divine and Human.
The Creation of Adam. Fresco, Sistine Chapel, Michelangelo, c 1512

In this passage, we begin to learn about human nature and emotions. God made a world that was "delightful" to humans. God provided the substance for life. God also had a special connection with humans. There was a mutual connection between the gift of life and the creation of a world to support life. Humans had the responsibility to care for that world. Genesis 2:15 says, "The LORD God then took the man and settled him in the garden of Eden, to cultivate and care for it."

At this point, the scripture writer says, in Genesis 2:19–20,

> So the LORD God formed out of the ground all the wild animals and all the birds of the air, and he brought them to the man to see what he would call them; whatever the man called each living creature was then its name. The man gave names to all the tame animals, all the birds of the air, and all the wild animals.

Pope John Paul II, now St. John Paul II, describes the magnificence and completeness of that first human. He says, "This man is male and female."[25] The Pope used the term "Original Tranquility" to describe this peaceful state in the garden.[26]

Next, in Genesis, we read of God's idea to bring creation to perfection. Genesis 2:18 says, "The LORD God said: It is not good for the man to be alone. I will make a helper suited to him." At the conclusion of Genesis 2:20, then into verses 21 and 22, we begin the final path to the fullness of humanity in Eden. The future of the human race was set in motion with the creation of woman.

> But none proved to be a helper suited to the man. So the LORD God cast a deep sleep on the man, and while he was asleep, he took out one of his ribs and closed up its place with flesh. The LORD God then built the rib that he had taken from the man into a woman.

Adam had already experienced his superiority to all the rest of creation. He alone had the ability to think and act to shape his destiny. He alone had an awareness of the divine. No other creature in the garden was like that. Now with Eve before him, Adam could see that Eve was like him in being superior to all other creatures. But Adam could also see what we see on our wedding day: the differences that make us, man and woman, that complete each other.

Marriage of Adam and Eve. National Gallery of Art, Jean Duvet[27].

At that point in Genesis 2:24, God explains how man and woman are to live together. God gives us the gift of marriage. God proclaims the goodness of what married men and women experience in their intimate lives as they become one body. "That is why a man leaves his father and mother and clings to his wife, and the two of them become one body."

This second story of creation ends with the statement of peace and goodness that was present that day. Scripture (Genesis 2:25) simply says, "The man and his wife were both naked, yet they felt no shame."

Think about this account in terms of what it is giving us. Is it a moral lesson or a science lesson? Clearly, it is a moral lesson. The words of Scripture tell us that the source of our being is God. Further, the human man and woman are superior to the rest of Creation. Man gives names to the plants and animals. Advancing the moral lesson, we read of man and woman created differently from each other but alike in superiority over the rest of the Earth. Finally, man and woman come together in a joining of bodies to become one. In the realm of morality, we can feel joy and shame. Joy comes from unity with God in the form of Original Innocence. Shame comes from defying God and wanting to hide. It is not the lack of clothing that gives us shame. It is the consciousness that we have done things counter to the Divine plan.

The Biblical moral lesson from Genesis 3, the account of the "fall," is that we live in a constant state of God and humanity in a covenant. Humanity is sometimes in harmony but often chooses its own way. Scripture presents the ongoing relationship of God and humanity as full of transgressions away from the will of God. God-given remedies follow these transgressions as we work our way back to harmony with God.

The story of the fall of humanity in the Garden of Eden established the reality that we humans like to have things our own way. We can be selfish in a way that opposes self-giving love. The words tell it like it is. We retained the ability, the power of intellect, that sets us above all other creatures. Whether you are a Biblical literalist who believes that Adam and Eve were historical figures or one who focuses on how, when, and why the words were written, the moral lesson is the same.

So far, this is all moral teaching and not history or science. The discovery of evidence that the Earth is older than 6,000 years came from things like fossils in various layers of the Earth that showed a natural sequence as the Earth developed. Science gave us that window. Science also gives us a window into how long human beings have been around. Some position this window as an enemy of faith. Until the mid-1800s, the delivery of a fully finished human at some point in the Earth's history was broadly accepted as literal and historical truth. Today people clinging to that belief identify as Creationists. However, most Christians today draw from science and Scripture to realize a much longer history for Earth and humanity.

II-2: Charles Darwin and Evolution.

The watershed event that led to a relook at human existence on Earth came through the work of Charles Darwin. Charles Darwin (1809-1882), in 1825, enrolled in medical school at the University of Edinburgh. Surgeries at the time were generally carried out without anesthetic or antiseptics, and fatalities were common. Darwin was traumatized by the crude reality of surgical practice that he witnessed and gave up his medical studies. He moved to Cambridge University to study theology. He was in no rush to take holy orders.

Charles Darwin

In 1831, Darwin signed on to a five-year voyage aboard the ship the HMS Beagle. During the voyage, Darwin traveled to remote regions of the world. He encountered life forms far different than he experienced in the British Isles. He saw birds with bright blue feet, sharks with T-shaped heads, and giant tortoises.[28] He collected plants, animals, and fossils and took detailed field notes. This experience shaped Darwin's theory of natural selection. The theory proposes that the "fittest" organisms with characteristics best suited to their environment are more likely to survive and reproduce. Gradually, these features may become more common in a population, and the species changes over time. When the changes are great, a new species can emerge.

One of Darwin's Discoveries: A Giant Exotic Tortoise.

Darwin gave us the Theory of Evolution via his book *On the Origin of Species* published in 1859. Darwin described how organisms evolve over generations. Darwin preferred the term "natural selection" to differentiate changes in species that occurred naturally versus human action, like genetic modification, that we know today.

Natural selection alters a species in small ways, causing a population to change over the course of several generations. When this happens over a long period, parallel with a geologic timetable, it is evolution.

The evidence supporting the Theory of Evolution comes from paleontology, the study of ancient plants, geology, and the study of ancient matter of the Earth, such as rock strata. The studies happen through fossil records, which show how species that existed in the past are different from those present today. These fossil records can be matched with geologic records to establish a timeline.

Darwin was a man of faith. He knew his ideas would be met with opposition. As he developed his theory and prepared for publication, he worried about how the religious community would receive it. Published in 1859, *On the Origin of Species* provoked outrage from some in the Church of England.

Darwin was quiet about his personal beliefs. His autobiography shows a gradual migration from Anglican Christianity to agnosticism.[29] The most insight into his faith comes from personal letters. In an 1879 letter to John Fordyce, an author of works on skepticism, Darwin wrote:

> [My] judgment often fluctuates.... Whether a man deserves to be called a theist depends on the definition of the term ... In my most extreme fluctuations I have never been an atheist in the sense of denying the existence of a God. — I think that generally (and more and more so as I grow older), but not always, — that an agnostic would be the most correct description of my state of mind.[30]

In other personal letters, especially letters to his wife, Emma, there is evidence of a couple seriously searching for truth. We do not have a record of all of Darwin's letters to his wife. But one letter from Emma to Charles is touching evidence of their loving, mutual search for faith through the science window.

> My reason tells me that honest & conscientious doubts cannot be a sin, but I feel it would be a painful void between us. I thank you from my heart for your openness with me & I should dread the feeling that you were concealing your opinions from the fear of giving me pain ... my own dear Charley we now do belong to each other & I cannot help being open with you.[31]

Since the days of Darwin, the Catholic Church has weighed in on the compatibility of Darwin's Theory of Evolution with faith. Pope Francis, in 2014 in a speech to the Pontifical Academy of Sciences, stated that Darwinian evolution is real. He also said that the creation of the Earth as a long process via the Big Bang is real.[32] The Pope said, "When we read about Creation in Genesis, we run the risk of imagining God was a magician, with a magic wand able to do everything. But that is not so," Francis went on to affirm that God "created human beings and let them develop according to the internal laws that he gave to each one so they would reach their fulfillment." Pope Francis was not breaking new ground with these statements. In 1950, Pope Pius XII wrote, "Catholics take no issue with the Big Bang theory, along with cosmological, geological, and biological axioms touted by science." Note the special mention of "biological axioms." This is the evolution of the biological existence we call human. Pope Francis reminded us that the Church has recognized Darwinian evolution for over 60 years.

Critics point out that Darwin's theory provided for a stand-alone system that does not require any guiding "rationality" or intelligent design. However, when we allow science to show the wonders of living creatures, especially the human body, we see the brilliance of the design we call human.

As we place science and Scripture side-by-side, we find alignment. Scripture says that God made man from the dust of the earth and breathed into his nostrils the breath of life. Think about this. These words say that man was formed from pre-existing material, the "dust of the earth."

The origin of the first humans was addressed in a public and official way by the Pontifical Biblical Commission in 1909. It said that the literal historical sense of "the distinctive creation of man" may not be called in doubt. But the Commission went on to say that the distinctive characteristic of humans is not a bodily element. The creation of the human soul made the origin of man distinctive.

In 1996, St. John Paul II addressed the Pontifical Academy of Sciences in a way that re-emphasized human exceptionalism while asserting that "Today, more than a half-century after the appearance of *Humani Generis,* new findings lead us toward the recognition of evolution as more than a hypothesis." On an earlier occasion, he had explicitly said that "from the viewpoint of the doctrine of the faith, there are no difficulties in explaining the origin of man in regard to the body, by means of the theory of evolution."

The Church brings faith and science together with respect for each. Faith and professed philosophical reasoning can come to a knowledge of God and many of his purposes through an understanding of created realities. This means looking fully through the science window to see those created realities. The Pastoral Constitution on the Church in the Modern World (*Gaudium et Spes;* GS) of the Second Vatican Council teaches that "methodical research in all branches of knowledge, provided it is carried out in a truly scientific manner and does not override moral laws, can never conflict with the faith, because the things of the world and the things of faith derive from the same God." The humble and persevering investigator of the secrets of nature is being led, as it were, by the hand of God in spite of himself, for it is God, the conserver of all things, who made them what they are" (CCC159, citing GS, no. 36).

This does not mean that there have not been conflicts between science and religion. In modern times, the scientific teaching of evolution has led to conflict within groups of Christians. The debate over evolution presents the choice between Biblical literalism and Darwinism or evolution. Some blend the two and recognize physical and biological evolution as the work of the divine Creator. The Catholic Church has continued to uphold the principle that there is no intrinsic conflict between science and religion as we consider human evolution.

In his 1950 encyclical (*Humani Generis*), Pope Pius XII applied this principle to the theories of evolution. He wrote, "The[Magisterium] of the Church does not forbid that, in conformity with the present state of human sciences and sacred theology, research and discussions, on the part of [people] experienced in both fields, take place with regard to the doctrine of evolution, in as far as it inquiries into the origin of the human body as coming from pre-existent and living matter" (no. 36). Pope Pius XII reiterated the doctrine that each human soul is immortal and individually created by God.

Pope John Paul II further commented on this question in his 1996 message to the Pontifical Academy of Sciences. The Pope acknowledged the scientific evidence in favor of evolution. But he went on to say that the spiritual dimension of the human person is of a different order and unique to humanity above the rest of creation. The soul makes the difference.

Here the difference moves into the realm of faith. That soul cannot be seen or proved by science.

Considering how science gives us a window into evolution and the duration of humans on Earth, we can draw from archaeology. The oldest known artifacts showing human action are some stone tools unearthed at Lomekwi in Kenya. These stone tools are about 3.3 million years old.[33] Other artifacts uncovered at Lomekwi include anvils, cores, and flakes.

Oldest Known Artifact of Human Action: Lomekwi, Kenya. Photo source: Smithsonian.com.

Another artifact dating far earlier than 6,000 years ago is a work of art. The Venus of Hohle Fels figurine is the oldest sculpture depicting the human figure. It dates to about 35,000 – 40,000 years ago. [34]

The Venus of Hohle Fels figurine. Photo source: Wikimedia Commons.[35]

We can see changes in human beings that fit Darwin's theory even in our own time. An example is the change in average height for American men and women in just the last 100 years. A study comparing height for Americans in 2012 versus 1912 shows a marked change. In 1912, American men averaged 5 feet 7 inches. In 2012 they averaged 5 feet 10 inches. Similarly, American women averaged 5 feet 3 inches in 1912. Now, they average 5 feet 4 inches. Studies show that being tall is associated with better health. There are also social advantages beginning with appeal in the mate selection process. Further, taller people get higher education and better income.[36] We tend not to think about natural selection playing out in real time before us, but here in America, it is happening as our human form changes.

II-3: When Did Pre-Human Beings Become Human?

Throughout the formal Church discussion of evolution, missing is a description of when the animal that we call human crossed into being fully human with an immortal soul. Reading the Church's assessment of the uniqueness of human beings, the line between humans and other created animals is the possession of a soul. Catholic evolutionists agreed that the origin of man, properly so-called, came only with the creation of the first human souls.[37] In his encyclical *Humani generis* (1950), which was addressed more generally to "some false opinions threatening to undermine the foundations of Catholic doctrine," Pope Pius XII said, "The evolutionary origin of the human body was open to discussion among experts, as long as the theological significance of the question was acknowledged."[38]

But agreement breaks down on the question of when, where and how these anatomically modern humans began to manifest creative and symbolic thinking. When did the humans first have the free will and insight to seek a connection with an eternal God?

Archeology shows that the first human ancestors appeared between five million and seven million years ago. With somewhat less certainty, most scientists think that people who look like us, anatomically modern Homo Sapiens, evolved at least 130,000 years ago from ancestors who remained in Africa. Their brain had reached today's human brain size. The physiology seemed in place for status as "human." But when did the spiritual character reach the point of a combined body and soul?

Dawn of Humanity

One view is that around 40,000 years ago the first evidence of abstract and symbolic thought appears in archeological findings. Human-like creatures were making more advanced tools and burying their dead with some sort of ceremony. This was the period when we first see human images depicted in art objects, like Venus of Hohle Fels. These are activities that a creature with a perception of the eternal and possession of a soul would pursue. Symbolic thinking is a form of consciousness that extends beyond the here and now to an awareness of the past and future.

One explanation for this advancement from animal to human is that it may have happened through a genetic mutation. The rewired brain allowed an advance in speech. Improved communications enabled people to communicate and jointly conceive the complexity of natural and social circumstances. They could manipulate culture. Such a jump seems like a transformation that fits Darwinian evolution.[39] It also fits the Biblical account of Adam and Eve, who had an awareness of the supernatural and unique ability to transform their surroundings.

Like the debate on the age of the Earth, the emergence of human beings is similar in both Evolutionist and Creationist thinking. The difference is timing. Important to say is that God's hand can be seen in either path to the humanity we are today.

We have a recorded partial history of human activity in Scripture. We believe that the oldest biblical text is the Hinnom Scrolls from the seventh century B.C.E. They were discovered in 1979-1980 by Gabriel Barklay in a series of burial caves at Ketef Hinnom. Ketef Hinnom is an archaeological site discovered in the 1970s southwest of the Old City of Jerusalem. When the silver scrolls were unrolled and translated, they revealed the priestly Benediction from the Book of Numbers 6:24-26 reading, "May Yahweh bless you and keep you; May Yahweh cause his face to Shine upon you and grant you Peace."[40] In those scrolls, we see the presence of faith.

This revelation was part of an evolution of faith that is resident in our Bible. The books represent a gradual unveiling of the truths of God and existence. In the earliest writings, there was no clear awareness of an afterlife. Later in Old Testament history, we see much more clarity about an afterlife. Even up to the time of Jesus, the evolution of faith and understanding of eternity was a work in progress. In the New Testament, we read of the tension between the Pharisees and Sadducees. The Pharisees believed in an afterlife. The Sadducees did not. Faith was a work in progress then as it is now. It was not all delivered as a finished package all at once. Today, our Church and its leaders continually provide a deeper understanding of God's eternal plan and our place in it. Among the tools used by theologians is science.

The very long age of the Universe and the relatively very short duration of humanity as we know it, should give us pause. In the context of the 13.7 billion years of the Universe, humanity's presence for 40,000 years is just a blip. The reality is that humanity is a tiny chapter in Earth's history. There is no reason to expect humans as we are to endure long enough to be more than a short stage in all of history going forward. Whether the exit of the human race on Earth comes via a game-changing event like nuclear holocaust, climate disaster, super-COVID, or God's declaration of Judgment Day, our time is short in the context of past and future history of the Universe. We must remember how precious this gift of life is. We must work as good stewards of creation in partnership with God. God is watching to see how we do as stewards of Creation.

II-4: Life: Odds Are, It's a Grand Design

The physicist Stephen Hawking ultimately denied the existence of God. Yet in his book, *The Grand Design,* he presents some strong arguments supporting a universe designed by an intelligent creator. A chapter in his book bears the name: "The Apparent Miracle." This title gives a glimmer into the mind of a man who saw evidence of a world that defied the odds of chance to become a place that supports life. At one point, he says, "Our solar system has other "lucky" properties without (which) sophisticated life forms might never have evolved."

One such condition is the shape of the Earth's orbit around the sun. Planets do not move in perfect circles around their star. In our case, the Earth moves around our star, the Sun, in a near-perfect circle. At its most distant, the Earth is 94.5 million miles from the Sun. At its closest, it is 91.5 million miles. The net result is an environment where temperature and radiation conditions are within the narrow range that is conducive to life. A couple of our neighbor planets follow a much more elliptical (elongated circle) orbit. Mercury is 200 degrees Fahrenheit hotter at its closest than its farthest approach to the Sun. If Earth had an orbit anything like that, the oceans would boil at the closest point and freeze at the farthest.[41]

Another chance or grand design occurrence is the position of our planet from the Sun. We are at a place that is a Goldilocks distance from the Sun: not too hot, not too cold, just right! Part of the perfection of the position of Earth is the perfectly balanced gravitational force that keeps our Earth in orbit around the Sun at the right distance. Earth is at the right point relative to the Sun and stays there. A little bit different one way or another, and Earth would be long gone into deep space.

Earth and Sun. The Right Distance for Life.

Finally, in discussing this grand design, Hawking tells us that the size of the Sun is good fortune for life on Earth. He says if the Sun were 20% larger (in mass), Earth would be as hot as Venus. If the Sun were 20% less, Earth would be colder than Mars.[42] The size of the Sun and our position relative to it within the Universe give the necessary conditions for life. As Michael Guillan says in his book *Seeing is Believing*, this is a very grand design that is wildly beyond any possibility of chance.

PART THREE

MYSTERIES OF SCIENCE THROUGH THE FAITH WINDOW

III-1: An Abundance of Mysteries.

In faith, we talk about mysteries. The Catholic tradition has the Rosary with its twenty mysteries that are really highlights of the Gospels. They begin with the announcement to Mary that she would bear the child, Jesus. The mysteries continue through the life and passion of our Lord, ending with his glorious resurrection, ascension, and his mother's assumption and crowning in Heaven. Each mystery is an event inviting us to ponder the wonder of God. As humanity advances, we discover more and more about mysteries. Sometimes what we learn clears up part of the unknown. At other times, discoveries add to an existing mystery or bring us a new one.

Neither faith nor science gives us a finished product when it comes to understanding our existence. We are left with some mystery by both. In Judeo-Chrisitan history comprehension about an afterlife developed over a millennium before the coming of Christ. It took Christianity 382 years to determine what books it should have in its Bible. Fifteen hundred years later, Protestant Reformers reconsidered that answer. It took Christianity nearly 400 years to land on its core beliefs about Jesus and put those together in the Creed. In the last hundred years, theologians working with science are helping us rethink what Heaven and Hell are like.

Mystery is a good term for any message of faith. We cannot see or tangibly prove most of the grand proclamations. We believe in components of faith, like the Christian Creed, because of things we see around us that give evidence of faith. We especially trust the revealed truth of the Bible. We also build from generations of witnesses before us who lived and died for those elements of faith. Our belief in a "Creator-God" is strengthened when we see the grandeur of the Universe and can imagine no other cause for its existence. We say God gives us grace to support us in life even though no one can show a handful of grace. We believe in the reality of God's grace from what we see in its apparent impact on others around us.

Things of faith, like grace, are similar to something like electricity. I cannot show you a handful of electricity, but I can believe it is there because of things I see that happen because of electricity. Lights go on, and appliances work because of this invisible thing called electricity. The observed actions cause me to believe electricity is there. When I see a long-married couple surviving all kinds of hardships, I see grace at work. In terms of the scientific method, grace is a mystery. In terms of our connection with the eternal, appreciation of the existence of grace is faith. But there is some overlap with methods of science. We believe in grace because we can see the effects.

In matters of life, whether a person is religious or not, belief in things beyond what we can see is essential. Science has delivered incredible evidence that calls for us to believe in things we cannot see. For the most part, we are expected to believe in the amazing discoveries of science.

Things like nuclear energy wrapped up in an atom are beyond our sight but the impact of the existence of nuclear energy is evident in things from generated power to weapons.

In those matters of science beyond our sight, and for most of us, the ability to comprehend means we sometimes need to take a "leap of faith." We do it when we go to a doctor and get a prescription. We do it when we hit the accelerator of our car on a freeway ramp. We believe that the unseen science is right and that we will enjoy the intended result. Religion and science have this in common.

Science has brought mysteries that are arguably even more difficult to comprehend than the mysteries of religion. We can find in the scientific discoveries of the last century a window into how magnificent and powerful our Creator is because of some of what science has shown us. We discovered nuclear forces with power beyond any imagined a century ago. We discovered a Universe that is vaster than imagined, pushing us to think about the infinite. We discovered incredible things about our own bodies and minds. We have discovered that things we thought were constant and absolute, like time, are not constant. We discovered that space may not be as empty as we thought. We discovered that there are many planets circling stars that could be similar to our Earth making us think about possible pods of life in God's Universe beyond Earth.

In the two sections ahead, the focus will be on mysteries. In the first section, Mysteries of Science Through Faith, the focus will be on a few mysteries that come from science and how they reveal God. Some of what we hear from science stretches the human ability to comprehend that they are real and open the mind to consider God as the designer of what we see. In the second section, Mysteries of Faith through Science, the focus will be on a few mysteries of faith that are also difficult to comprehend. The hope is to discover ways that science is adding to our attempts to understand those mysteries of faith.

In presenting mysteries from two angles, it will be apparent that some of the "truths" we see from science are more difficult to believe than many of the mysteries of faith. In both sections, I offer evidence about how faith and science can partner in a willing mind to gain an ever-deeper understanding of life and eternity. We really can deepen our faith in God by looking through a science window.

Whether it is religion or science, many of the wonders before us are beyond a layman's ability to see. But in each case, we can ponder an important part of life that we believe to be true. We believe some because science says so. We believe in others because religion says so. Either way, as we consider amazing discoveries and revelations, I encourage considering how those accepted truths, from science or faith, give us an ever-increasing appreciation of God.

These sections encourage thinking about these wonders in a personal way. The goal is to find even more awe and wonder in the Universe around us. Foremost, as we ponder these wonders that push toward infinity, we can use those wonders to look deeper at God and our place in infinite eternity.

III-2: Science Mysteries: Tiny Particles, Empty Space and Immense Energy.

We begin consideration of the mysteries of science reminded of the 13.7 billion years of Creation discussed in the preceding chapters. As we think about how the Universe began, we consider time and space that possess a magnitude beyond imagination. At the same time, our discoveries guide us to ponder the infinite micro-work of a divine craftsman far more skilled than the paramount watchmaker.

As we look at the infinitely large and infinitely small, we are looking at part of the mystery of time and space. In the simple Genesis creation account, time and space are plain and simple. Twentieth-century science moves us much farther to awareness of what infinity might look like and how we fit in. Time is not as fixed as we thought and extends far beyond the literal limits described in Scripture, computed to be 6,000 years. Similarly, the boundaries of space are far beyond the early Biblical model all enclosed in the dome. These are just a sample of many topics that come from an intersection of science and faith.

This is not a science book, so I will only hit the tops and talk in simple language that might not satisfy a genuine physicist. My aim is to help you (and me) to be impressed with Creation and the marvelous hand behind it. We can look with wonder at the infinitely large and find a grand designer.

Likewise, we are brought to awe as we look at the infinitely small with complexity far beyond comprehension.

Topics considered in this part include:

- The complex atom.
- Incredible energy within and among us.
- The vast universe of time and space: We are so tiny!

III-3: The Complex Atom.

Out of the many wonders of modern science, I begin with a discussion of the atom and its makeup. Within the atom are the tiniest building blocks of matter. The atom is the basic building block of all things—living and inert. The details of the atom we see today were invisible for all but the last 130 years of human history. Think of the leap of faith needed by even scientists to accept atomic existence as these new truths of science were revealed.

Fifty-some years ago, I was taught about the matter we are made of. A core high school chemistry lesson was that all matter is composed of atoms. Those atoms are made up of protons, neutrons, and electrons. In my classroom model, the protons and neutrons were clustered in a tight package of spheres in the center of the atom called the nucleus. The model showed the central nucleus surrounded by spherical electrons circling close in. The electrons stay close because of the electromagnetic attraction between the positively charged protons and the negatively charged electrons. Everything is neat and compact. The atom is made up of solid material tightly held together without much empty space. I could see it in my classroom model! That was my level of belief in atomic structure until a few years ago.

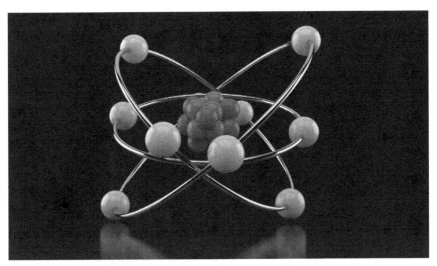

The traditional atomic model.

Physicists today tell us there is so much more. There are smaller building blocks that make up protons and neutrons. There are forces and particles of force that hold those building blocks together. There is also a huge amount of apparent empty space inside an atom. Furthermore, the story of atoms is not just about the stuff we call mass or matter. Energy is a huge part of the internal atomic story. In fact, the internal energy within the nucleus is far more powerful than gravity or electrical attraction. All of this can be traced back to the beginning. Whether it is a single act of a Creator triggering the Big Bang or a random event, we can see the wonders of creation in the atoms that shape us.

Nuclear physics tells us that the smallest building block of matter that we know of now is a tiny thing called a "quark." Quark is a weird name for something that is the foundation of all matter: living or inert. The word comes from a line in a James Joyce novel, Finnegan's Wake, "Three quarks for Muster Mark."[43] Anyway, that is the name these tiny particles have.

Without going much deeper, each proton or neutron is made up of three quarks. Some quarks are called "up," others are called "down." The quarks are held together by an immensely strong force that physicists call "strong force." Clever! But there is more. There is a strong force that holds quarks together and holds protons and neutrons together. This strong force is made up of things that resemble elastic bands. Like an elastic band, the farther apart the particles are, the stronger the force. These things of nuclear strong force are called "gluons." This is not Star Trek. They really exist and are called gluons.

PROTON   NEUTRON

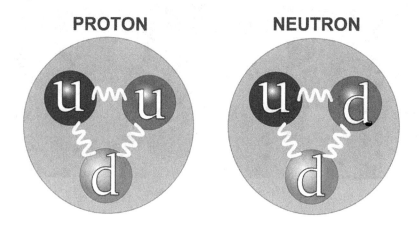

Quarks within a proton and neutron. Credit: Wikipedia Commons

Indeed, a quark is tiny. To get an idea of how small this is, begin with a single molecule of water which is one ten billionth of a meter. Then, look inside the molecule to the nucleus of a hydrogen atom, which, along with oxygen, makes up water. That hydrogen nucleus has one proton that is 10,000 times smaller than the water molecule. Then, look inside the proton to find the three quarks that make up the proton.[44] The quarks are 10,000 times smaller than the proton. The University of California at Berkely puts this in context: "Suppose we amplify a quark to the size of a grain of sand (one-thousandth of a meter) and amplify a man by the same factor, then this man would be so big that he could swallow the entire solar system like an egg!"[45]

A look at a hydrogen atom is a good place to appreciate the wonder and power of creation. Most hydrogen atoms have one proton and one electron. Unlike the plastic model in my high school chemistry lab, the proton in a hydrogen atom is not just a solid sphere. It is a collection of three tiny quarks held together by immensely strong gluons and loads of empty space.

Going back to creation, the study of the Big Bang reveals that at the instant of creation, intense heat and pressure compressed all the matter and energy of the Universe into a package smaller than a grain of sand. At first thought, squeezing so much matter into a small space seems impossible. But now we know that matter is a collection of quarks and other sub-atomic particles. In the discussion of the relative size of an atom, we know that most of the volume of an atom is void of particles. If a proton were a little wider than a baseball infield, the quarks would be the size of green peas. One pea would be at home plate. A second pea would be at shortstop and the third at first base. Moving the same image to the relative size of the water molecule, the baseball infield-size proton would be within a single molecule with a radius extending about 400 miles from Chicago to Minneapolis. There is a lot of empty space in which to squeeze the matter of the Universe as a setup for the next big bang.

There is much more detail to this subatomic picture. Without going deeper into detail, the point of this discussion is that the makeup of all the matter around us, including our bodies, is far more complex than imagined fifty or more years ago. The deeper we look, the more impressive the makeup of everything around us is. Yes, the words of Genesis inspire us with awe for the God who can, at his will, deliver life as we know it. But much more impressive is a Creator who can assemble something as basic as a water molecule that science has shown us is far from simple. That molecule is made up of tiny bits relatively far from each other held together with immense energy.

Science gives us the bridge from the complexity of a chemical molecule to the composition of life. A century ago, scientists showed that we are made up of cells. One hundred years ago, we learned that cells are comprised of chemical molecules. Then we learned that molecules are made up of atoms. We learned that atoms are composed of protons, neutrons, and electrons. Now we see those nuclear components made up of even smaller parts: quarks. That is what we are made of, and it is immensely complex.

We continue to discover how complex this masterpiece and the world we live in is. We get to see this through science. As science guides us to see deep into our makeup, we cannot find a mistake. The perfection of matter and life is beyond chance. It is a marvelous design.

III-4: Incredible Energy Within and Among Us.

Amazingly, mass and energy are interchangeable. Albert Einstein's equation can describe this interchange:

$$E = mc^2$$

In the equation, E is energy, m is mass, and the "c^2" part is the speed of light times itself (squared). The speed of light, "c," is a huge number: 186,000 miles per second. Taking the c times itself yields a phenomenally huge number. So, by this arithmetic, a tiny bit of mass is equivalent to a huge amount of energy.

This energy in and around us was unheard of in the days when Scripture was recorded. The symbol of power was the strength of a horse. In Psalm 147:10, "He takes no delight in the strength of horses." Today we can go to a car dealer and find a car with 400 horsepower. In Scripture times, energy was known as heat from a fire or the radiance of the Sun. The closest thing to the conversion of mass to energy was putting wood in a fire or grain into an ox.

As science helped society advance, we increasingly found ways to use the energy in the created matter around us. Much of this has been done in the last 200 years. Fuels advanced from wood to minerals, first coal, then oil and gas. These advances utilized chemical energy, which adjusted combinations of atoms without changing the atoms themselves. For example, in combustion, oxygen and carbon combine to form CO^2 and release heat in the process. During the burning of wood or coal, we start with a certain amount of carbon and end with the same amount of carbon. The atoms and the mass within them do not change.

But combustion does not approach the magnitude of energy contained within the nuclear structure of elements around us. In a nuclear reaction, a small amount of mass is converted to a large amount of energy. This is the power of the Einstein equation describing the energy released when a small amount of mass is converted to energy. Remember the speed of light times the speed of light factor. Whether it is an instant release via a weapon or a timed release in a power plant, the reaction is beyond anything our ancestors could imagine. This small amount of mass to deliver a large amount of energy is why nuclear fuel for things like submarines makes sense. Subs can carry very little fuel to go a long way. This is an example of how science has given us a look inside our tiniest parts. As we look, we see the energy of a magnitude that most of human existence could not see.

Bringing this back to our practical life, nuclear energy is a reality in good and scary parts of life. The obvious scary part is the power of a nuclear weapon. History showed the destructive power of such a weapon at Hiroshima and Nagasaki. The Cold War showed that the weapons used in Japan were babies compared to what man has constructed since then. Nuclear weapons are rated by force in terms of tons of TNT, a powerful chemical explosive. The Hiroshima bomb had a force of 15,000 tons of TNT. The bomb had a diameter of only 28 inches! The most powerful weapon ever detonated was known as Czar Bomba, detonated by the Soviet Union in 1961 and rated at 50,000,000 tons of TNT.[46] Yet this bomb was small enough to be carried on a plane.

A visit to a military museum provides a look at what such a weapon looks like. The image below is of a thermonuclear (fusion or hydrogen) weapon in the U.S. arsenal. It is small enough to fit on a cart but carries over twenty times the power of the Hiroshima weapon. It is 13 inches in diameter. A military man told me that the fuel within such a weapon is smaller than a basketball. How can a tiny package deliver so much force?

Photo source: Wikipedia B61 nuclear bomb casing,
MAPS Air Museum, North Canton, Ohio

The story is inside the atom and directly tied to the nuclear furnace that brought us the Universe. For most of us, this is a mystery. For most of human history, this energy was invisible. All along, it was there, but who knew? Rocks containing uranium were findable in mining districts but did not look any more potent than any other mineral rock. But physicists have come to understand the source of this energy within those rocks, minerals, and elements. That energy has been captured for terror, such as weapons, or good, such as power generation. The physicists unlocking this energy also give us a window into the majesty of things that happened in the process of Creation. Fusion in a thermonuclear bomb is the same fusion process that happens in the Sun.

Recalling the structure of the atom, physicist Ralph Treder, PhD, explains, "Nuclear fission, via splitting of nuclei, releases Coulomb energy. Nuclear fusion, the joining of nuclei, releases "strong force" energy accumulated by the natural attraction of nuclear particles.[47] Large nuclei have a conflict between the strong force (attraction of nuclear particles) and the Coulomb force (repulsion of like charges). Imagine 92 uranium protons (like-charged and repulsive) jammed together in a tiny nucleus that binds them via gluons." In a nuclear fission reaction, some of the strong force within the uranium atom is unleashed in the form of neutrons escaping at high speed. The resulting elements after fission, including the escaped neutrons, have a slightly lower total mass than the heavy uranium atom had. A tiny amount of mass is converted to energy. The mass reduction becomes energy, true to Einstein's equation.

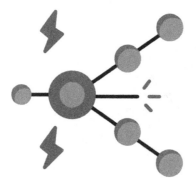

Fission of uranium 235 into the lighter elements, krypton and barium, with the release of three neutrons and energy.

A fusion reaction starting with the smallest element, hydrogen, releases even more energy. Our Sun is the poster child for this fusion process. As hydrogen atoms are fused to become helium, heat and light are generated. Here on Earth, we feel the heat 93 million miles away from the Sun. Many religions looked to the Sun as a god because of its role in sustaining life and as a source of energy beyond anything on Earth. Christians look to the Sun as a similar source of life but believe it to be a product of God's work and plan of creation.

Thinking about the magnitude of this energy within the atom, a comparison of energy from various fuels is helpful. We could start with the great power of Scripture time: the horse. In a way, a horse uses chemical reactions as grain molecules are broken down within the horse's body into other combinations like exhaled CO_2. Energy is released through the work of the horse. Within the senses of Scripture writers were other chemical reactions occurring in things like fire. For most of human history, chemical reactions were the limit of any imagination of energy in the stuff around us.

Science of the 20th Century revealed that there is much more mystery in Creation than imagined. The science window opened to show us incredible energy within the atom. The difference between the energy from chemical (fossil) fuels and nuclear is startling. Fission or splitting of heavy atoms is the process used in nuclear power plants. The fission of 1 gram of uranium or plutonium delivers as much energy as 3 tons of coal or about 600 gallons of fuel oil. Think about this. A piece of uranium about the size of a pencil eraser can deliver as much heat as a truckload of coal or oil.[48] The nuclear process of the Sun, fusion or combining of hydrogen nuclei to form helium, delivers 3 to 4 more times the energy of a fission reaction. A gram of hydrogen fusion fuel can yield as much energy as over 2,000 gallons of fuel oil.[49] What we do with this power is up to us. We can use it to destroy the world with weapons and war or save the world through carbon-free, efficient power generation. Where did this power come from? Creation of the Universe. It was there all along, but we never saw it.

For most of us, the immense energy within the atom is a mystery. Even after I work the math, I still struggle to appreciate the energy within a tiny bit of nuclear fuel. I believe that energy is there because of the impact attributed to it described by scientists. This mystery is as baffling as any matter of divine faith. It takes faith in science to accept this energy potential as real. Faith in God is similar. We have faith in the Divine because we see so many signs of its truth in the everyday world around us. Our observation of the world moves us to believe. All we have to do is look.

I close this section with a thought to drive home the mystery within us when it comes to energy within the atom. This calculation has no practical application other than to make the point about how vast mysteries are in life described by science. These wonders are products of a grand designer whose work we never completely understand. There are amazing things, energy, and powers in everyday matter around us. Most of the time, we cannot see them. But science shows us that they exist. These wonders are in the stuff of Creation. What we believe about them came through science and what we see is incredible.

The average American weighs 180 pounds. Water makes up 60% of a man's weight (55% for women). So, the average American body includes 108 pounds of water. Water contains two hydrogen atoms and one oxygen atom. The hydrogen atoms make up 1/9 of the weight of water. So, the average American body includes 12 pounds of hydrogen. Now, here's the interesting nuclear part. One in 6,400 hydrogen atoms is heavy hydrogen. Heavy hydrogen is a hydrogen atom with at least one neutron. The presence of one or two neutrons in a hydrogen atom provides the substance for a fusion reaction as nuclear fuel.

Based on the occurrence of heavy hydrogen, we can calculate the amount of nuclear fuel that we carry within us. I suspect that few people reading this imagined carrying around any nuclear fuel. Since the average human body has 12 pounds or 192 ounces of hydrogen, by the normal occurrence of heavy hydrogen in nature, we have about 0.03 ounces of heavy hydrogen within us. That is 0.85 grams. Back to my comparison of energy from oil and coal to nuclear reactions, each of us has enough heavy hydrogen within us to match the heat from about 1,700 gallons of oil. It is part of how we are put together. Hot flashes, anyone?

Fortunately, it takes an extremely high temperature to trigger a fusion reaction. Scientists tell us it takes millions of degrees to trigger such a reaction. So, nuclear fuel is safe within us. Welcome to the intensity of creation.[50] In the context of mystery, this energy presence within me is much harder to accept than mysteries of divine faith.

SEEING GOD THROUGH THE SCIENCE WINDOW

None of this power within the atom was known 150 years ago. Humanity lived nearly 2,000 years after the last book of the Bible was written, with no clue about this energy within the matter around us. This power was part of Creation, but no one knew until science opened the window. Except for the most knowledgeable physicists, I suspect most of us struggle to imagine the power within a tiny bit of uranium or fused heavy hydrogen. We believe that power is there because we see signs of that power in nuclear power and weaponry. We believe in it because we have faith in the scientists who know those things.

The challenge we have as seekers and believers is to gain a "we can bet on it" level of confidence in the reality of the Divine. Many accept $E=mc^2$ as a given fact but struggle to find God. Those are the folks I encourage to look out of the science window to find God in the mystery around us. Is it any more of a stretch to have faith in God, who told us we could have the power to move mountains with a mustard seed-sized bit of faith, than to believe in the power of the mustard seed-sized bit of heavy hydrogen within us? (Matthew 17:20-21).

We can look at the world around us to see wonderful things humans can do with a little faith. Christians can look to the simple carpenter's son who lived in an out-of-the-way corner of the Roman Empire who now has over 2 billion believers who shape their lives after him.[51] As we read in Acts 5:38-39, authorities debated what to do about the early followers of Jesus. They said, "So now I tell you, have nothing to do with these men, and let them go. For if this endeavor or this activity is of human origin, it will destroy itself. But if it comes from God, you will not be able to destroy them; you may even find yourselves fighting against God." With two billion followers today, I profess that we see the power of God evidenced in this unlikely world of 2 billion believers.

III-5: The Vast Universe of Time and Space. We Are So Tiny!

Up until a century ago, awareness of our place in time was in the context of the 6,000 years of Earth's existence. Scripture reminds us that our life is short and quick. Psalms 90:9-10 says: "Our life ebbs away under your wrath; our years end like a sigh. Seventy is the sum of our years, or eighty if we are strong; Most of them are toil and sorrow; they pass quickly, and we are gone." In early Jewish history, there was little awareness of an afterlife. In that era, the belief was that we human beings are born, work hard, live a short life, and are gone. In those words, the context of time was the existence of humans in this world and nothing else. After death, souls existed in a state known in Hebrew as Sheol or in Greek as Hades (CCC633). These terms were used to describe the abode of the dead. In the earliest models of the Universe, Sheol was the underworld beneath the dome and the land. Souls were resident there, whether evil or righteous. Death was the end.

As pre-Christian faith history moved ahead, awareness of an afterlife developed and became pronounced in late period Old Testament Scripture. At the time of Jesus, Jewish faith leaders were divided on whether an afterlife existed. The Pharisees held belief in the afterlife. The Sadducees did not. In either case, all were certain that time moves on without interruption and that time applies to every human being. Until the last few hundred years, that movement of time totaled about 6,000 years. Time was important to describe history, the order of creation, and expectations about life.

Within the confines of this planet, one constant in human thinking has been time. The daily cycles of the Sun define a day in a way that does not vary from one person to the next. Time is still important in our context today, but the accepted magnitude of time is vastly greater than two centuries ago. Thanks to the window science opened to creation, we understand that our Universe has existed for billions of years and humanity, with the form of body and soul as we know it, for 40,000 to 100,000 years. This is humbling, looking backward and forward. Backward we see the evolution of the human mind and body amidst a grander evolution of society. Writing has been around for maybe 4,000 years and language for maybe 40,000 years. But these time spans are minuscule compared to what science shows as the duration of our Universe.

Whether we can imagine time as having billions of years of history or a lesser number, time has been long thought of as constant. A day is a day, no matter who or where you are. So we thought until Einstein told us that time is not constant. He told us if we were twins and you traveled to a distant galaxy very fast, and I went nowhere, you would come back younger than me. Einstein postulated that for this time variance to happen, travel speeds must be very fast and distance very far.

Up until Einstein's ideas, scientists and everyday folk could plainly see a world of four dimensions: length, width, height, and time. A stick measuring 12 inches long is 12 inches long for anyone else who credibly measures the stick. Even more certain, one hour in a day is the same no matter who is measuring or where they are. The idea that any of those measures had a "relativity" factor that could yield a difference was beyond belief.

As we consider time, we must also look at distance. It is in great distances that we start to find immense measures of time. In these considerations, we use a measure that combines time and distance. We use the term "light-year," which I explained earlier. As we connect science to faith, we start to see what infinity might be like in a way that our distant ancestors could not imagine.

First, regarding distance. From the early belief that all was contained in a dome with the sky above the earth and the oceans, with Sheol below, we now see more. Our understanding of the expanding Universe gives a look at how very far the far reaches of the Universe are in both time and distance. There is no known edge to the Universe. Space spreads out infinitely in all directions like an expanding balloon. As we look deeper, we see many galaxies in the Universe, some dwarfing our own.[52] Recently, using the Hubble Telescope, scientists found what they believe to be the most distant star. It is now 28 billion light-years from Earth. The star was born within the first billion years after the Big Bang.[53] The light we see from this star took 12.9 billion years to reach Earth. What astronomers see as they view this star is how it looked nearly 13 billion years ago. Gazing at this star we see a Universe that was only 7% of its current age.[54] When it comes to distance, the star's current location, 28 billion light-years from Earth, is a big number.[55] It would take light emitted from that star today twice as long to reach us as the total time elapsed since creation. The Universe is very big!

For most of us, the time spans and distances we deal with are short compared to cosmic dimensions. We, 21st-century humans, are limited within our lifetimes to travel very short distances in the context of the Universe. We hope to travel to Mars. Current technology would allow us to get to Mars in seven months covering 300 million miles.[56] Mars is only twenty-seven light minutes from Earth. The nearest star, Proxima Centauri, is 4.25 light years away.[57] Any imagination of travel at a speed to cover light-year spans is beyond any credible science fiction.

Where science fiction and science do intersect draws from Einstein's theory of relativity, wherein he stated that time is relative. Einstein is the man who told us that the amount of energy and mass in things around us is not fixed. We used to think mass and energy were separate things, but Einstein showed that they are connected and relative. Likewise, he stated that time is not constant.

According to Einstein's theory, as we increase our travel speed away from Earth, our aging slows. If we go fast enough, approaching the speed of light, we can reach long-lasting youth compared to those who stayed on earth. At this point, there is no way we can do that. However, the truth of Einstein's theories has been verified through observation.

A place where the variance of time has been detected and subsequently matters to all of us is Global Positioning System (GPS) technology. GPS devices calculate a position based on communication with at least three satellites in Earth's orbit. As most of us see, these devices are incredibly accurate down to the measure of feet. To do this, the satellites must be incredibly precise in the dimension of time. They work based on atomic clocks. The atomic clocks are on satellites traveling in distant space orbits around the Earth at 8,700 mph. GPS satellites fly at an altitude of approximately 12,550 miles.[58] Einstein's theory says that for satellites, there is a difference of seven microseconds, or seven millionths of a second, each day compared to a stationary object.[59] In order to maintain pace with Earth clocks, atomic clocks on GPS satellites need to be adjusted seven microseconds each day. These GPS devices bear out the variability of time as they travel great distances at great speeds. Einstein was right. Time is not fixed. It is relative.

When we talk about distances of light years or speeds approaching the speed of light, we need a playground far bigger than Earth. As we see amazing power and wonder in things like relativity, our scale expands beyond Earth to the Universe. The humans recording Scripture, or interpreting Scripture for most human existence, had no concept of these wonders. Now we can see in ways that they could not how our world and presence are tiny in the scope of distances and speeds we see today. On the other hand, we are still limited. We can see only so much in our Universe. We can detect things about distant stars and planets, but we have no reasonable chance in our lifetimes to get anywhere close to a physical encounter with them. We must take these concepts through faith in the scientists who reveal them. Scientists tell us how our GPS devices work. We see what they do and believe in the science.

Such distances and what we see from those distances give a window into God's Universe that is far greater than imagined a century ago. We know that the Universe we see exists and know it got there somehow. We know this because we believe what scientists tell us. In the last 100 years, science has given us a deeper look into that window. What we see moves us closer to awe and wonder about the power of God. We are starting to see what infinity in time and space looks like. We see more and more the truth of what we cannot see with our own eyes and even senses.

Whether it is science or faith, we take what we observe and carry it into what we believe. We rely on observations and witness accounts from those who have gone before us. Witness accounts from our ancestors were limited to what they could understand. We read those accounts in our family diaries, old science books, and the Bible. When we convey the same truths today, our words would be somewhat different because of our place in history and the context we have are different. That is why we need to go beyond the "literal" to get the whole substance and revelation from Scripture. We must use all we have, including scientific, literary, and historical methods, to understand the full meaning of Scripture. The window of science is critical to advancing our understanding of God and our place in his eternity and Universe. When we look around us, we can trace it all to a beginning. Whether we call it the Big Bang or Creation, we still get back to, something had to make it all start.

PART FOUR

MYSTERIES OF FAITH THROUGH SCIENCE

IV-1: Looking Through the Science Window at Mysteries of Faith.

Humanity has learned much about its origins and existence thanks to science. In some ways, scientific discoveries make faith easier. Discovering the immensity of the Universe or the complexity of life brings an appreciation for a grand designer. The findings of science can humble us when we see our place in time or ponder where we come from. Each new discovery adds more appreciation for God as the creator. We see life as a Divine masterpiece.

In contrast, some use these discoveries to dispute the existence of God. They claim that much of what we read in Scripture and believe in our religions is a product of the human appetite to explain the unexplainable. They work hard to explain every detail of our existence through natural laws. They do not make room for God. Some such people are well-meaning and honest seekers of truth but unable to reach a standard of proof to satisfy their search. Others lack an open mind to the possibility of a divine explanation for the unexplainable.

In the previous section, we considered some incredible mysteries of our physical world brought to light by science in the last century. Those discoveries help us see the wonder of God. In this section, we ponder some mysterious matters of faith, considering what science has shown us about our natural world that can help us grow in faith.

I save the elephant in the room until the end of this book. By elephant, I mean: Does God exist? The topics in this section assume the reader does believe in God, or at least has a leaning that way.

Some of the topics to be considered are:

- What is God like?
- What does God look like?
- What and where is heaven?
- How does God relate to billions of people in a personal way?
- Are there interventions over natural law?

IV-2: What is God Like?

The image of God depicted in pictures generally is of an old, bearded man, usually visible mainly as head and shoulders. He has a human face and rarely speaks. He is infinite in wisdom and power. He looks downward toward us. He can do anything and cause anything. Generally, people look upwards to address him. Our connection is personal, one-on-one. But really, based on that typical image, if we met somebody looking like that on the street, many of us would move to the other side.

The Catholic Catechism reminds us that our ability to fully understand God will take us only so far. An attempt to find God purely with logical means aiming for a solid "proof" picture will leave us short. The Catechism says, "Even when he reveals himself, God remains a mystery beyond words: 'If you understood him, it would not be God.'" (CCC230).

What we can find with our senses are attributes of God.[60] Science is a significant source to feed our senses when it comes to finding God as his actions reveal his attributes. Among the attributes, we find that he:

Is self-existing without beginning or end. He is without a maker or external cause. With our senses showing us that everything around us needs some source of being, only such a God can be the source our senses seek.

Never changes. We see this via our senses in the Natural Order around us. The laws that Newton, Einstein, and others defined for us are not changing. We can find no exceptions. We see that evidence even back to the beginning of time.

Is all-powerful (omnipotent) and all-wise (omniscient). The immensity of the Universe, starting with the action of the Big Bang, shows a power that is infinite. We are starting, through science, to understand the reality of infinity. We are beginning to see a wisdom that is unmatched in even the most perfect human system. The perfection of the Natural Order without the need for revision throughout the history of the Universe argues for infinite wisdom. He got it right the first time.

Is loving, just, and merciful. This world is a good world. The gift of our humanity equipped with an ability to connect with our maker is a love story. Looking again to the natural order, it is just and merciful at its most basic level. Yet part of the love story is that we have free will to choose to act in concert with that love and order or choose our own way.

In the early days of the space race, Atheists believed that when we got to space, the "ultimate up," we would not find God. The absence of God and heavenly palaces would confirm that he did not exist. Indeed, cosmonauts reached orbit in 1957 and failed to find any person that looked like God. The Russian cosmonaut Gherman Titov, who followed Yury Gagarin, the first human launched into space, reportedly returned to Earth with a simple, Soviet-style message: "I looked and looked and looked, but I didn't see God."[61] A famous Kremlin propaganda poster produced at the time featured an image of a cosmonaut floating in space and the slogan, "There is no God."[62] What they and subsequent space travelers found was a breathtaking view of our planet that inspired even non-believers to appreciate the presence of God.

Soviet propaganda poster by Vladimir Menshikov: There is no God.

IV-3: What Does God Look Like?

In the artist's depiction of God as an elderly gentleman with long white hair and a long beard, he looks serious and is usually by himself. Much of our image of what God looks like can be sourced back to Scripture. "And he said: Let us make man to our image and likeness. …. And God created man to his own image: to the image of God he created him: male and female he created them." (Genesis 1:26-27).

As we look at ourselves, we conclude that since we are made in God's image, he must look like us. What that passage from the Book of Genesis tells us is that as man is created in God's image and likeness, we are different from the rest of Creation. The passage is specifically directed at the creation of man, not any other part of Creation. It is intended to differentiate humans from all other created things and creatures.

What a physical description misses is that God is Spirit, not a physical thing. What makes man in God's image is spiritual. We have free will. We have the ability to know God. Our senses and imagination take us to an active role in shaping the world we live in. Likewise, our senses and imagination let us activate the theological virtues of faith, hope, and love that bring us to God. We have an immortal soul connecting this world to the next.

IV-4: What and Where is Heaven?

The traditional answer is "up there" at the end of some path, behind pearly gates in the clouds. The traditional faith-based image is a place of great rest and happiness. A feature in many artists' drawings is apparent calmness. All in all, after the trials and difficulties of life, arrival in Heaven is worth whatever Earthly sacrifice we need to make to get there. It is the ultimate reward.

Heaven Above

These images bring questions about what Heaven is really like. An eternity of idleness does not seem appealing. Also, what about the crowd? Scientific studies of the growth of the human population say there have been around 105 billion people on Earth since the start of humanity.[63] Any reasonable percentage of that population would provide quite a crowd in the Heavenly space. Where are most of those people in the artists' pictures of a peaceful Heaven? That does not sound like an environment of eternal rest.

So, what is Heaven, really? My first answer to most who ask is, I don't know. I have not been there. But from everything I have read in Scripture and learned from others in faith, here is what I think. Pope John Paul II said that the essential characteristic of Heaven, as well as Hell and Purgatory, is that they are states of being of a spirit. They are states of the human soul rather than places. This language of place is, according to the Pope, inadequate. We cannot look "up there" or anywhere else for Heaven in a physical sense.

In July 1999, the Pope said that Heaven is the fullness of communion with God. "It is our meeting with the Father which takes place in the risen Christ through the communion of the Holy Spirit." [64] The Catechism of the Catholic Church teaches, "This perfect life with the Most Holy Trinity, this communion of life and love with the Trinity, with the Virgin Mary, the angels, and all the blessed, is called 'heaven'. Heaven is the ultimate end and fulfillment of the deepest human longings, the state of supreme, definitive happiness" (CCC1024). None of these definitions mentions a place or direction.

Given that Heaven is a spiritual state, it is no wonder that the cosmonauts did not find it. Pertinent to understanding Heaven is our look at science and the findings about our Universe in the last century. God is not bound by some space somehow layered around Earth. As we say the Universe is infinite, we are even more correct in saying Heaven is infinite. An indication of this is how the Church renamed the Feast that used to be called "Christ the King." The feast, which occurs on the last Sunday of the Church year, is now called the "Solemnity of Our Lord Jesus Christ, King of the Universe." The Church seems to be looking out the same window as scientists. All see how extensive Creation is beyond this planet. There is also a hint in that name, King of the Universe, that in case any life is found beyond this Earth, Christ is King of that, too. On this last point, few scientists give much credence to the existence of life beyond Earth. It might be easier for people of faith to see the possibility of life beyond what we know today, honoring the power of an infinite and eternal God. He is the King of the Universe. Who are we to limit him?

IV-5: How Does God Relate to Billions of People in a Personal Way?

This is a question from people who are advanced in their faith life and seeking a deeper understanding of God. They have come to believe in God. They actively look to him in prayer. But one day, they wonder, I am just one of a planet full of people talking with God. I'd like to think he's talking personally with me, but what about the several billion others doing the same thing? How does he do it?

Over a billion people looking to God at once. How does he hear us?

There was a movie about twenty years ago called *Bruce Almighty.* The plot of the movie centers around a man who is fed up with how God is handling things and thinks he can do better. God gives him his chance. Quickly Bruce is inundated with requests from desperate people seeking God's help. Soon, Bruce is overwhelmed and resorts to saying "yes" to every request, thinking he will make everybody happy. He soon discovers some serious flaws in that mode of operation. He finds that the omniscience of God must be infinite to avoid the catastrophes that saying yes to all creates. The point we can take from that is that there is no super-computer or other tool that can do a good job of being a personal god to everyone. The detail of how God answers a million prayers at once cannot be contained in any physical description.

God is outside of time. That has been a longstanding Church teaching. Science now shows us that even in natural law, time is not a constant boundary. Time that prevented Bruce Almighty from doing God's work is not a constraint on God. God is fully spirit without any of the limits of a physical body. As I look up to God from my Michigan home, someone in Australia is looking up to him, too. But thanks to being on the other side of the Earth, the Australian is looking in the opposite direction. But we are both looking to Heaven to a spirit without shape or limits who can connect with us.

Jesus, on several occasions, showed this spiritual character. His appearances after the Resurrection in a locked room (John 20:19-31), apparently going through material walls or closed doors, show us a spiritual form. So does his appearance on the road to Emmaus, where his disciples did not recognize him. (Luke 24:13-35). Then there was the Transfiguration, where Jesus was suddenly before three disciples in a different form. With him were two men long dead, Moses and Elijah. (Mark 9:2).

Thanks to the discoveries of the last century, we are invited to ponder the wonders of our physical life, like empty space within an atom or seeing an image today from a star as it appeared billions of years ago. These facts of modern science defy our ability to see and understand. Compared to these wonders, it takes less of a stretch to imagine a God who is not limited by time and space. Such a God can do what no human can imagine doing: answer millions of prayers in a day.

IV-6: Are There Interventions Over Natural Law?

The topic is miracles. According to the Catechism of the Catholic Church, a miracle is "a sign or wonder such as a healing, or control of nature, which can only be attributed to divine power. The miracles of Jesus were messianic signs of the presence of God's kingdom" (CCC547). The Church teaches that miracles are a sign of wonder attributed to divine power and God's mercy, such as control of nature or healing from a grave medical condition.

The Church requires that the miracles submitted for a person's beatification and canonization (being identified as a saint) be miracles of healing. To recognize a cure as a miracle, the event must withstand a thorough examination by doctors approved by the Church. The cure must be spontaneous and lasting. It must not be the result of medical intervention and cannot be explained by medical science.[65] This is a very tough screen to pass and depends on science as a key part of any declaration of "miracle."

For an act to be considered a miracle by the Catholic Church, it must meet specific requirements set forth by the Church:[66] The event must be:

Attributable to divine power: One of the most important requirements for an act to be considered a miracle is that it be directly attributed to divine power. God is the only one who can be the cause of a miracle. Any incident that may have stemmed from created causes, such as nature or man, cannot be considered a miracle. While the wonderful effects of extraordinary acts of man or nature may be beneficial and marvelous, they do not qualify as miracles.

Beyond the abilities of nature: Another important aspect to consider is if the effect is beyond nature's capabilities. First, a miracle surpasses created powers in the produced effect. While natural processes create life in humans, they cannot do this in somebody who is no longer alive. The raising of Lazarus is an example where Lazarus was fully recognized as dead. Yet he came out of the tomb. That was a miracle.

Additionally, the subject rather than the effect defines the miracle. While God can cause an effect that nature also can produce, he does so in a way nature does not. For example, it is natural for a fever to pass. Surviving a disease, even against strong odds, is not a miracle. However, the cure can be miraculous if the ailment leaves by command or prayer when medical science offers no hope.

Beyond nature's order: A miracle must be God's direct work and beyond all created powers. This relates to the other requirements. What is seen is a connection between a faithful petition for divine intervention and a result that is not possible through any earthly processes. The result is unexplainable within natural law but is explainable as an answer to explicit prayer.

Seemingly extraordinary: A miraculous event is extraordinary, meaning it is contrary to the ordinary course of events. For example, a person aching to be a parent and not able to conceive may defy odds and science to give birth. In most cases, it is wonderful but would not stand the "miracle" test. While the creation of human life is awe-inspiring and a divine gift, God decrees that creating life is part of the normal course of events. Sometimes that happens to people who, for years, have been told they are infertile. But there are cases where fertility could be determined as impossible through extensive medical tests. Yet birth happens. Evidence may show that the impossible birth happened after the direct petition for divine intervention. That is extraordinary enough to be a candidate for recognition as a miracle.

The ability to sense: Finally, a miracle needs to be perceptible by the senses. A literal interpretation of the Bible leaves no doubt in miracles as they are recorded as events that people saw. In the Christian Bible, Jesus works many miracles. We read about the disciples doing miracles in God's name. These were signs and wonders for a purpose, including bringing others to see and believe in God. Anyone living a Catholic life has an awareness of miracles through the works of men and women recognized as saints. Miracles are meant to prove God's revelation and must be marked with a divine character that can be sensed. Even those who are not believers are forced to consider the truth of miraculous action by God in such events.

Believing in miracles can be easy, a no-brainer, or very difficult. Personal experience can lead a person in either direction on a particular event. One person may see the cure of a person previously diagnosed with an incurable disease as an intervention in the natural order and a miracle. Another may see the same event as a product of the natural order but somehow beyond the skill of the diagnosticians to understand.

Those who have experienced tragedies despite extensive prayer are left to wonder about the truth of miracles. They can further wonder if they believe in miracles; what is the selection process God uses as he allows miracles? I know a woman who lost a daughter in a plane crash. The plane was missing for an extended time. There was hope that somehow it landed in the ocean and its passengers survived. Thousands of prayers were offered, but the wreckage was found with no survivors. She says, "I believe in miracles but don't know who gets them."

Someone who is not a literalist in reading the Bible must look to observed events and search for interventions in the Natural Order. Faith tradition assures us that miracles happen, but there remains an interior investigation to discern and ask, have I ever seen one? Some have. Some have not.

In many ways, the recognition of miracles is a circle. People who have not come to believe in miracles rely on their senses that, even after good conscience efforts to believe, they cannot say they have ever seen one. Such a person can look at a highly unlikely event and see a possibility of a one-in-a-huge-number chance that the result could happen naturally. While they cannot document the natural cause of the result, they see the possibility that the result could happen without suspension of natural law. Others who believe in miracles see the same event but give way to faith that divine intervention brought the otherwise impossible result. For one, seeing is believing. They see God's hand in many things. They may even use the word "miracle" for things that are not, by the truest definition, miracles. A more proper name for some of these benevolent answers to prayers would be blessings because the result does not require any overturning of the laws of nature.

For those of faith, belief can be the cause of seeing. They see God's hand in everything. Sometimes such people of faith can overlook heroic actions by doctors and others who bring deliverance from pain. They miss the gifts given via talents and generosity within fellow humans. Certainly, a skilled friend is a gift from God through his or her life, skill, and character. But these saving acts are not interventions in natural law. They are not miracles. That is why the Church has precise criteria for recognition of an event as a miracle. In the broad population, the criteria are less clear.

There are people of sincere heart in both camps: the people who see and thus believe and those whose belief is the foundation of seeing. Such good people are not as far apart as it looks. It is impossible to see what is in another's heart. The disciples in the Upper Room after the resurrection included both dispositions. The story of Thomas and his so-called doubt brings that home. Thomas saw all that Jesus said and did, yet he did not jump to accept a miracle without evidence that it was true. When he saw, he believed. Thomas and his fellow disciples carry the title of saint even though they had different roads to belief. (John 20:19-31).

Thomas' path to belief is just like the Church's path to belief in a miracle. Struggling to believe is not a sin or obstacle in faith. When the struggle is done with an open heart an extraordinary degree of belief can be the result. We can use modern personality type analysis to depict Thomas as a type who depended on his senses. His fellow disciples were more inclined to depend on intuition. Our world and churches are filled with people of both types. Faith is a gift, but we also need to open our eyes to honestly see and believe. The path will be different for each one of us. We are not all wired the same. A problem in our churches is that we don't always recognize those inherent differences among us. We are quick to judge based on what we feel and see after filtering observations through our own predisposition and personality lens. We are challenged to be more like Jesus. He looked past differences and met people where they were. The road to belief is different for everybody.

PART FIVE

JOURNEY TO BELIEVE

V-1: Seeing is Believing and Believing is Seeing.

Considering the discoveries of science describing the formation of the Universe, Earth, and humanity, it is easy to see a Creator at work who pulled the trigger to put this in motion. We can see that as this multi-billion-year sequence was initiated, physical laws were put in place to govern things like motion and force. Science shows us these laws and shows us that throughout all this time, those laws were perfect from the beginning with no need for amendment. Certainly, we are left with abundant mysteries from science and religion that challenge our comprehension, but scientific observation and faith lead us in the same direction. In science and religion, we come to believe in things unseen based on things we can see.

Michael Guillen, PhD, in his book, *Believing is Seeing,* states odds on the Universe being formed through random chance in a way that would support life.[67] The number he presents based on attributes necessary for life is beyond comprehension. He says the odds of all the circumstances coming into place to allow life in this Universe are one in 10 to the 120th power. That's 10 times 10 times 10...120 times. Huge. Unimaginable!

When someone is searching to believe in God, there are challenges. We cannot see God. We cannot really comprehend infinite power or infinite existence. The grandeur of God presented by religion and Scripture exceeds what we can directly see. There is also the struggle of how such a powerful creator could have a personal connection with us individually.

Yet, the wonder of Creation presented by science is at least as incredible and impossible for most of us to grasp as comprehending an unseen God. Science tells us that something like humans existed for over a million years. Most of those years passed before we showed signs of our fully developed form, especially the social and spiritual characteristics we recognize as uniquely human. Science says that somehow, about 40,000 years ago, the time was right within the course of evolution for those spiritual characteristics to be present. For humans that live an average of about 85 years, these time spans stretch our ability to comprehend. Trying to imagine our presence of 85 years in the context of billions of years makes us less than a blip in time. When we feel the humility that comes with that "blip," comprehending an unseen God within the wonder of Creation is easier to believe.

Where religion adds to science is revealing a purpose for our human existence in this long physical and biological evolution of the Universe. Most, if not all, religions state the creation of humanity as a purposeful product of Divine action. We are not just an accident of some super-long-shot chance. Judeo-Christian faith tells us that humanity was being shaped from creation to love and serve God. We were fused together in a covenant of love.

These religious beliefs are not in opposition to science. They are supportive and parallel. Neither can be proven beyond all doubt. Both have been accepted on logic and faith by thinking people throughout recorded history. The sweet spot for belief, whether it is looking at what religion presents or science, comes when we draw from both. When we look deeply at what science is showing us, it becomes much easier to see the necessity of a grand designer. Whether it is a grand design by an intelligent Creator or an amazing result of a series of low-probability events, Earth, as it exists as the third planet from the Sun, is a wonder. Some might say it is a miracle.

V-2: The Human Appetite to Find God in the World Around Us.

The study of societies that existed before the time of Christ or before any exposure to the Christian Word yields traditions quite close to Judeo-Christian beliefs. These histories that emerged before any contact with Christian missions show how the heart and mind of humanity are drawn to God naturally. Somehow, someway, human hunger comes up with the same general beliefs despite widely different cultural backgrounds. This should tell us something about the truth of the existence of God as the Creator.

The following includes a discussion of faith within two cultures that were outside the view of the Europe-based Church. First, is a look at faith in Egypt. Formal society and religion in Ancient Egypt predated Judeo-Christian records by at least 2,000 years. Second, is a look at the Hawaiian religion before any exposure to Judeo-Christian scripture or Western thought.

Egyptian Tradition. Dr. Jennifer Houser Wegner, Associate Curator in the Egyptian Section at the Penn Museum, wrote about the Egyptian story of creation. An excerpt from her writing describes the beginning of creation. Note the combination of light and dark. Also note the role of the serpent, similar to Genesis.

> The sun god spent the twelve hours of the night traveling in the underworld, ultimately merging with Osiris, the primary funerary deity. The journey was treacherous, and the sun god faced his enemy, Apophis, a serpent who threatened him as he traveled in his solar boat nightly.

The Egyptian God Ra

Another of Ra's important roles was as a creator god. The sun's reappearance on the horizon at dawn each day was a symbol of the re-creation of the world. However, Ra was not the sole creator god in Egyptian mythology. The Egyptians had several elaborate myths describing the origins of their world. Each of these creation stories was centered at a different city in ancient Egypt.[68]

Ancient Egyptian creation stories are the earliest religious compilations in the world.[69] Egypt of the Pharaohs became solidly in place as a society around 3100 B.C.E. with the unification of Upper and Lower Egypt. Upper and Lower describe the position along the Nile. At that time, over 1,000 years before Abraham, formal religion in Egypt was apparent. There was an awareness of the afterlife and powers beyond this world. We have credible documentation of Egyptian society and religion from well before the first biblical manuscripts were written. Our records tell us that the realization of a Creator God was embedded in Egyptian society well before Joseph brought the Word to Egypt. God was at work in human hearts.

Judeo-Christian history intersects with Egyptian history, with the arrival of Joseph in Egypt around 1900 B.C.E. and the Exodus around 1200 B.C.E.[70] The first Biblical manuscripts were written sometime between 1450 B.C.E. and 1000 B.C.E. It is evident that the earliest Biblical manuscripts and accounts were verbal recollections rather than historical records. The earliest biblical event that can be matched with certainty to secular history is from the second book of Kings (2 Kings 17:3). The historical evidence comes from an artifact that can be seen in the British Museum in London. It records King Ahab of Israel and King Adad-idri (Ben-Hadad) of Aram taking part in a joint venture against King Shalmaneser III of Assyria at the Battle of Karkar in 853 B.C.E. This date is the earliest Old Testament date that can be corroborated from a non-biblical source.[71]

Despite the lack of detailed historical names and dates in Scripture, science and faith do intersect in establishing an approximate date for Exodus. In Genesis and Exodus, Egyptian Pharaohs are identified merely as "Pharaoh." Traditionally, the Pharaoh of the Exodus is believed to be the 19th dynasty Pharaoh Ramesses II because the Hebrew slaves were forced to build the Egyptian city named in the Bible as Raamses.[72] Raamses II reigned from 1279 to 1213 B.C.E.

A traveler today can see evidence of this faith in the monuments along the Nile. The ancient Egyptians had many creator gods and legends, but there was one creator god who stood out. The earliest god, Ra, emerged and gave rise to Shu (air) and Tefnut (moisture), from whose union came Geb (earth) and Nut (sky), who in turn created Osiris, Isis, Set, and Nephthys. In all these accounts, the world was said to have emerged from an infinite, lifeless sea when the sun rose for the first time. The Egyptians had the cultural skill of writing to record what they believed. What we know of their beliefs is a combination of writing, spoken legend, and architectural monuments. In their hieroglyphics, we can connect with their beliefs. Hieroglyphics provide a written record of Egyptian belief in a Divine Creator.

Hieroglyphics describe life in Ancient Egypt.

The different stories of creation, Egyptian and Judeo-Christian, have some elements in common. They all hold that the world rose out of the lifeless waters of chaos. The Sun was also closely associated with creation. The Egyptian story of creation shares the belief that there was a divine force behind creation. There was the emergence of light from darkness. The Earth was formed, rising out of the sea. This is just like the mental picture of the dome surrounded by water in our Bible.

The Egyptian story of creation was based on observation of the world around them. Somehow, without any exposure to the scriptures of the Judeo-Christian tradition, they could detect the presence of God in ways matching the inspiration of Western religions. The names given to the deities were different, as were the details. But inspiration led the Egyptians to know that there is more to our existence than pure chance. The evolution of the Egyptian faith came from their use of the science window encompassing three millennia B.C.E.

Hawaiian Tradition. The Hawaiian Islands are the most isolated geographic entity in the world. The island chain is far separated from Asia and even more separated from the Holy Lands of the Middle East. But God's revelation and inspiration are evident.

Every culture in the world has a way of recording history. However, the Hawaiian language had no written form. History was passed down orally through songs, chants, and dance. During her imprisonment following the overthrow of the Hawaiian monarchy in 1897, Queen Liliuokalani wrote down the words of this creation tradition in a work called the Kumulipo. This chant records the Hawaiian creation story. It starts with the creation of the Universe and human beings and ends with the genealogy of royalty.

Queen Lilioukalani

Early Hawaiian religion was polytheistic, with primarily four deities: Kāne, Kū, Lono and Kanaloa. According to the Kumulipo, in the beginning, there was darkness inseparably connected to an invisible intelligence. This darkness is Papahānaumoku, the mother of Gods, the Earth, and the underworld. And then there was the creative light from Wakea or sky father.[73] Think of the parallel to Genesis chapter 1. "In the beginning, when God created the heavens and the earth and the earth was without form or shape, with darkness over the abyss." "Then God said: Let there be light, and there was light." Also, think about the similarity to the early understanding of the Universe as a dome with an underworld. Somehow, human minds were being inspired to believe in similar explanations for our existence.

The Hawaiian creation story in the Kumulipo links the aliʻi, or Hawaiian royalty, to the gods. The Kumulipo is divided into two sections: night, or pō, and day, or ao, with the former corresponding to divinity and the latter corresponding to humankind.[74] Again, there is a similarity with the description of creation in Genesis when it comes to the emergence of man and then woman.

As the Hawaiian culture and religion evolved, places of worship and sacrifice, like the heiau, became important. Eventually, in the 19th century, Christianity took root. A diligent comparison of the Hawaiian tradition with Christian theology reveals significant similarities. Knowing the similarities helps us understand how Hawaiian royalty was attracted to the Christian faith.

Royal Temple by Jean-Pierre Norblin de La Gourdaine[75]

In her introduction to the Kumulipo, Queen Liliuokalani recognizes the "analogies between its accounts of creation and that given by modern science or Sacred Scripture."[76]

People of faith and science should notice these early accounts of creation as examples of faith and science working in tandem to understand our existence. Many cultures developed traditions of belief based on observing the natural world and knowing that there must be more. God has no boundaries of time or place. In these stories, we see God reaching far beyond the boundaries of any church.

V-3: Christianity Expands its View of the Universe Through Discovery.

Discoveries, especially the discovery of the New World in the fifteenth century, caused the Catholic Church to adjust its stance on who can be reached by the saving hand of God. This is a case of the science of exploration and discovery having an impact on faith. Prior to the discovery of the Americas, it was easy to say that there is no salvation outside the Catholic Church. This stance drew from St. Augustine and others. The known world was Europe and its immediate neighbors. Everyone in that geography theoretically had the chance to hear the Gospel. Those who heard the Gospel could elect to either believe or stand outside the Church. Each person was understood to have that conscious choice. Thus, if you were not in the Church, you were assumed to have, by personal election, moved outside the Church. With the discovery of the New World, there was the moral question of the salvation state of the people who had never heard the Word of the Gospel. Were they automatically doomed through no fault of their own? The discovery of people like the Hawaiians, who had not heard the Word, were examples that challenged traditional thinking within the Church.

The fifteenth-century Council of Florence reaffirmed that "none of those living outside the Catholic Church" "can become sharers in eternal life." But that was about to change. Theologian Francis A. Sullivan, in his book, *The Church We Believe In: One, Holy, Catholic and Apostolic*, draws from the Council of Florence and connects to the moral eye-opening delivered from mission work. [77] He says a transformational philosophy emerged from the Jesuits. They looked mercifully at those who lived outside the institutional Church through no choice of their own. The Jesuits gave new life to the call to bring the Good News everywhere.

With that challenge to conventional thinking, there started to be some redefinition of the "no salvation outside the church" stance. That change was an evolution on its own. Even in the 1950s, mission societies in the U.S. sought money from Catholic school students to save "pagan babies."

With the Church's Second Vatican Council, a monumental change occurred within the Catholic Church. Pope Paul VI in his letter, *Lumen Gentium*, brought good news and hope that God does not exclude anyone from the opportunity for salvation. The call is universal: "All men are called to belong to the new people of God" (LG13). The message of *Lumen Gentium* was a faith reaction to what was observed through the secular science window.

We can be humbled by history. As we debate points of faith, it is easy to see what we see and take it to be a complete read of reality. But history shows that our human state of wisdom is never finished. As humanity advances, we see more and more of the wonders of Creation. Faith and the Church continue to be a work in progress.

There are lessons in this for people of faith and science as we understand our Universe and Eternity. The search for meaning and truth needs faith-based theology and the natural sciences. Each discipline will continue to do what they have done for several thousand years: Advance the knowledge of who we are and where we fit in time and space.

V-4. Arguments for God Science Style.

We finish this reflection on seeing God through the science window with the ultimate question. Does God exist? Overwhelmingly, humans throughout history have said "yes." The answer to the affirmative comes from observation of the physical world supplemented by whatever inspiration the Divine provides.

I propose that people of good conscience ponder this question more than is externally apparent. In this personal matter of finding interior peace with what we believe, each person's road is unique. It is impossible for any of us to know completely what is in another's heart. Backgrounds differ, experiences differ, and challenges differ. Even different personality types face a disparity of challenges along this path in understanding as two people attempt to understand the same experiences. Think about the "doubting Thomas" experience. Those with personality preferences to seek answers through feeling and intuition face a different path from those who are naturally gifted with logic and observation as their strengths.

In a world full of judgments, exploration of beliefs can be difficult. Societies with a "state church" or strict religious code leave no room for open exploration. Even in open societies, churches can impose a limit on open exploration of beliefs. Those who hold views not fully aligned with the church will be subject to social pressure, potential shunning, and exclusion. I know many people in my faith tradition suppress questions in the interest of belonging and fitting in. Only in very intimate settings do these thoughts and questions surface. Science fields carry some of the same limits. If a researcher is inspired to explore dimensions of a natural question that carries a political overtone, they can expect to do so without grant money and academic advancement. Think about some social issues or climate patterns where society knows the answer and does not welcome challenges.

So, how do we get to the point of knowing, really knowing the answer to this question of: is God there? Many have tried to give us that answer. The most enduring set of parameters toward "proof" of God comes from Saint Thomas Aquinas. This great theologian of the 13th century published a masterpiece that stands today as arguably the most recognized set of proofs for the existence of God. Aquinas' five statements of proof stand with enduring credibility, similar to Sir Isaac Newton's laws of motion. They have survived the test of time. They have survived scientific and faith discoveries and massive changes in the world.

Saint Thomas Aquinas, between 1265 and 1274 C.E., presented five proofs of God in his major theological work, *Summa Theologica*.[78] Aquinas' five proofs were:

1. **The Argument from Motion:** Whatever moves is moved by something else. This is similar to the substance of Newton's Laws of Motion, which would not be stated until 400 years after Aquinas. Aquinas concludes that there must be a First Mover. This is God. Newton agreed, including the "god" part.
2. **The Argument from Efficient Cause:** Because nothing can cause itself, everything must have a cause. Without a first cause, there would be no others. Therefore, the First Cause is God. Creation stories from ancient civilizations get the same answer.
3. **The Argument from Necessary Being**: Nothing can come from nothing. Something must exist at all times to create a continuation

of things. This is God. Once again, creation accounts from many cultures come to the same answer. In the Egyptian account, the starting material is simply called chaos.

4. **The Argument from Gradation:** There is a gradual increase in complexity among created objects. The substance of our world ranges from the simplest inorganic matter to complex organisms. This is a statement that Darwin would find accurate in his work on evolution. There must be a being of the highest form of good. This perfect being is God. Darwin left much of the movement to the complex to chance but still kept open the possibility of God.

5. **The Argument from Design:** All things have an order. Aquinas proposes that all things have a purpose. Here Aquinas makes a major assumption to support his proof. He assumes the order of the Universe could not have come from chance. He concludes that there must be a designer for the Universe, and the designer must be God.

Aquinas' proofs have stood the test of scrutiny for almost a millennium. The challenging reality with these proofs is, that they require a degree of faith, or acceptance of the existence of God, to make them stand. The arguments for "first mover," "necessary being," or "perfect being" all make sense and can be proven by logic as an order of things. The problem for someone trying to prove the existence of God with these statements is that they require that God be the principal in each. There is no other obvious candidate. It is like having a trial where there is no direct evidence that the accused did the crime, but all others are eliminated as suspects. Thus, the last left standing is determined to be responsible.

The answer to the "who's responsible" question, for most, comes from faith. For others, it comes because no one has thought of a different answer that can withstand a proof test under the scientific method.

V-5. One Scientist Looks for God Without Satisfaction.

In recent years, the great theoretical physicist Stephen Hawking wrote about whether God exists or not. While many focus on Dr. Hawking's statement in his final book, saying that God does not exist, there is evidence that he diligently tried to find a different answer. In that last book, *Brief Answers to the Big Questions,* he wrote, "The question is, is the way the universe began chosen by God for reasons we can't understand, or was it determined by a law of science? I believe the second," wrote Hawking. He went on, "If you like, you can call the laws of science 'God,' but it wouldn't be a personal God that you would meet and put questions to."[79] At his end, Stephen Hawking believed that there is a "grand design" to the Universe but that it has nothing to do with God.

Dr. Hawking was not always an atheist. He grew up in a home described as "nominally Christian" or "Intellectually Atheist."[80] As a university student, he actively debated religion with his colleagues. In 1988, he spoke of God in his book *A Brief History of Time* and said that if physicists could find a sound "theory of everything," they would understand "the mind of God." He once believed that we would one day discover this unifying, coherent theoretical framework, like God, that explains the Universe.[81]

Over the years, he did not find solid evidence of God that would pass his proof process as a scientist. His later statements show his transition from search to denial.

> "I'm not religious in the normal sense. I believe the universe is governed by the laws of science. The laws may have been decreed by God, but God does not intervene to break the laws." (BBC News Interview, April 26, 2007)

> "One can't prove that God doesn't exist, but science makes God unnecessary." (In an interview on September 7, 2010)[82]

In this series of statements, we can see a continuum of thoughts that are very personal. There is no mention of a partner in this search. There is no mention of anyone filling a spiritual advisor or director role. Finally, there is no mention of any expression of hope. It is sad that this great man did not see the possibility that the end of his life might open the door to new discoveries.

V-7. Other Scientists Find God as a Source of Hope.

Other people of science see the same amazing Universe as the basis for faith in God. They see new discoveries offering more evidence of a grand Universe designed with precision beyond chance. The wonder of science gives them the foundation to conclude for the existence of God. One of the most moving examples I have encountered comes from a neurosurgeon, Dr. W. Lee Warren.[83] Dr. Warren has expertise in treating people with a horrible brain tumor, glioblastoma--multiforme. In medical science, the average survival after diagnosis of this condition is usually months.

In his book, *I've Seen the End of You: A Neurosurgeon's Look at Faith, Doubt, and the Things We Think We Know,* Dr. Warren tells his story of the difficulty in treating patients with this disease that almost always brings near-term death to the patient. Thus, the title of his book. He describes the emotional and spiritual challenge of seeing symptoms or lab reports pointing toward the tumor and knowing that it is almost certainly going to claim the patient. The scientist in him says, "This is it. I've seen the end of you." Yet he gives the human side of reconciling what does he say to the patient and family desperate for hope? How do we pray for something that we know likely will not happen?

Through it all, Dr. Warren presents a life facing extreme challenges to faith yet growing in faith. Dr. Warren describes his struggle between faith and observation. He records being with patients and families desperately trying to preserve the lives of loved ones, sometimes at enormous cost. He has witnessed the desperate prayers of those patients and loved ones. Dr. Warren documents the challenge of moving forward with confidence when his specialty is treating people with a "disease that God almost never heals."[84]

Dr. Warren is a brilliant doctor and scientist. He experienced the trauma of war, served in Iraq, and suffered personal loss, including the tragic murder of his son. Professionally, he shares his personal challenge of the tension between "God can heal our disease, and (his) knowledge— This disease is 100% fatal."[85] He brings to the table the concept of "doubt." An important part of Dr. Warren's lesson is the difference between doubt and absence of faith.

Doubt is not the denial of faith. Doubt is part of seeking with open eyes. Doubt is not a sin when it leads us to greater faith. An honest hunt for the truth can result in a stronger, more mature commitment to Christ. Some of the greatest faith is seen in those who came to believe as adults, often after great doubt. Honest skepticism that is at least open to the possibility of God allowing God to do great things is a natural and good thing. Dr. Warren's testimony shows how doubt is part of spiritual honesty. He presents many cases of people of faith faced with questions like "Why did God allow these horrible things?" as he viewed the horror of Iraq. Or "Why did not God answer my prayers and save my loved one?" Or "How can I believe what I cannot see?" Yet we see that there is joy to be found in allowing doubt to lead to faith. Read his book, and you will see what I mean.

There are things that can help us survive the challenges of doubt. We see that in Dr. Warren's description of his challenges and growth. First, he did not walk the path of challenge and doubt alone. He had the support of a loving wife. He connected deeply with a chaplain, Pastor John, at his hospital as a spiritual confidant in both easy and difficult times. He continued in prayer even on days when he must not have felt like it. Most of all, at various points in his narrative, he describes hope, particularly hope in things not seen.

V-8. A Leap of Faith Brings Hope.

From what I read about Dr. Hawking and Dr. Warren; they were/ are brilliant men. I believe they are good, sincere men. Both have an extraordinary grounding in science. They observe the same physical world. Yet, one concludes that God exists. The other concludes the opposite.

This brings us to realize the place for a leap of faith. There are limits to what we can see. In our scientific world, we believe that quarks exist as basic building blocks of matter, even though no one has ever seen one. We believe that the speed of light is a universal speed limit, even though we have never approached it. We believe (and hope) that we will find cures for things like glioblastoma--multiforme tumors. We believe we can take a risk and marry someone who will love us for life. People of science believe many things that cannot be seen.

"For by grace you have been saved through faith, and this is not from you; it is the gift of God." (Ephesians 2:8-9). There is only so far we can go on the road to the scientific proof of God. From there, it takes faith. Scripture promises that the gift of faith is there for us. A mystery remains, why do some seem to get more of this gift than others?

Even among great saints, some struggle while others just have it. In modern times, Saint Mother Theresa is an example of one who struggled. She spent much of her life struggling with faith, losing the presence of God, and even thinking that she did not believe in God. We know this from letters she wrote released after her death.[86] In a 1962 letter to a Bishop and friend, Saint Mother Teresa of Calcutta remarked, "People say they are drawn closer to God-seeing my strong faith. Is this not deceiving people? Every time I have wanted to tell the truth, "that I have no faith," the words just do not come." In that same letter, she described how she made it through the dark moment. "Deliberately, I took the Rosary and very slowly, without even meditating or thinking, I said it slowly and calmly. The moment passed."[87] She continued with total dedication to her work and obedience to Jesus and the Church. She never quit praying. She never quit seeking. However, for her, doubt was a long-term challenge. Anyone struggling with matters of faith can look to Mother Teresa and know they have good company.

Mother Teresa's example connects with some lessons learned from Dr. Hawking and Dr. Warren as they searched for God. Dr. Hawking seemed alone. He did not have a spouse or life companion. He did not have a spiritual advisor to help at times of crisis. He did not include an expression of hope in his writings about the possibility of more. In contrast, Dr. Warren is married to a woman who is a partner in faith as well as a partner in life. They even work together professionally. Like Dr. Warren, Mother Teresa had her faith community and numerous spiritual advisors who helped her carry on in faith.

Belief is not a solo sport or a one-game event. We need others. We need community. We need persistence.

V-9. For Those Who Just Don't Know, Pascal's Wager.

One scientist who found a practical way to nudge us toward belief when uncertainty reigns is Blaise Pascal. Blaise Pascal was a French mathematician, physicist, inventor, philosopher, and Catholic writer.[88]

He is famous for his "Pascal's Wager." Pascal's Wager is the name given to an argument Pascal proposed for believing or for at least taking steps to believe in God. Pascal's argument is aimed at people who are skeptical but trying to believe. He does not push to the point of arguing that God exists. He logically argues that we ought to believe in God.[89]

Choices and Consequences of Pascal's Wager		
	God Exists	**God Does Not Exist**
I Believe in God	Worldly gains from a life of virtue. **Infinite gain** in the eternal presence of God.	Some earthly cost from forsaken vice. Offset by the gains of virtue. **No eternal cost** or awareness of loss.
I Deny God	**Infinite loss** from eternal separation from God and awareness that personal choice is the cause.	Some earthly pleasure and cost from a life of vice. **No eternal cost.** No awareness of gains or losses.

Pascal looks at the consequences of the option for faith in God compared to denial. He concludes that we should wager that God exists because it is the best bet. Pascal maintains that we are incapable of knowing whether God exists or not. Reason cannot settle the answer in an absolute "I can prove it" way. However, since all of us will face the end of earthly life, we must get selfish and weigh the consequences of the decision. If we accept God and God indeed exists, the payoff is huge. Scripture and faith traditions of all sorts present that. If we deny God and are wrong, those same scriptures and traditions, not to mention Dante in his *Inferno,* tell us of the terrible price of that denial. If we are wrong in our belief and God does not exist, we will never know. Any sacrifice we make in this world in the name of faith will mean nothing since we will never be sad over what we missed. So, for the mathematician Pascal, the answer was obvious. Belief in God, even if you cannot prove it to yourself, is the right choice.

What Pascal is offering is the challenge to have hope even when we cannot prove that the hope will be fulfilled. This type of search and commitment to faith is evident in Mother Teresa's diaries. Pascal's argument makes it obvious that, on one side, we can consciously refuse to believe in an unseen God. We can toss any possibility of God aside. That means abandoning any form of hope for something good beyond this life. For people who make that choice, there is nothing good to gain beyond, perhaps, some sensuous enjoyment in this life. Or we can choose to believe in the unseen God, with the potential for infinite joy. This seems like a slam dunk case to take a leap of faith.

While the grace of faith is far better than settling for Pascal's logic, anyone struggling with faith should consider this argument. In believing in God, there is much to gain and, in the end, nothing to lose. Those of faith assure us that God will give us the grace needed to see and believe. It may not come as fast as we like, but it will come.

V-10. Faith, Hope and Love: Virtues Drawing Us to God.

As human beings, we do our best to understand ourselves and those around us. Some are good at this, some not so. Part of that effort, even for an atheist, is wondering about what lies beyond this life which raises the question of our relationship with God. Contemplating the eternal leads mostly to some form of faith or lack thereof. Most people, based on the percentage of the world that claims some form of religion, come to a level of faith in the Divine. A 2010 survey showed that 51 percent of people in the world believe in God. Only 18 percent did not, and 17 percent remained undecided.[90]

With uncertainty, some dimension of skepticism or doubt, we need a path to a working belief in God. By "working," I mean a level of belief that considers the human struggle to believe in something that is short of absolutely provable. Mother Teresa can be our model to give us a license to say, okay, I'm struggling.

Scripture and people of faith before us give us the path. The path is to let God work through a life of faith, hope, and love. These are virtues or habits of living that lead us to a good end. In the Catholic Church, faith, hope, and love are called theological virtues. What gives these virtues the theological label is that they build our direct relationship with God. Faith allows us to connect with God at some level of confidence. Hope allows us to focus on our ultimate destiny with optimism that we are going somewhere good. We know that the work of virtuous living is worth it. Love gives us the foundation to act for good. Often the word charity is used interchangeably with the word love in describing this virtue. In St. Paul's beautiful love letter, his first letter to the Corinthians, he looks beyond this life to what will last. In 1 Corinthians 10, he says, "When the perfect comes, the partial will pass away." Shortly after that, in verse 13, he adds, "Faith, hope, love remain."

Virtues are about finding a way in life that gives true happiness. Virtues are good habits that guide us to make good choices, live morally, and find happiness. We can live our lives in faith strictly from obligation. But God tells us he wants us to be happy. We hear that point in the Beatitudes: the "Happy are they" series. The theological virtues of faith and hope give us reason to know that the result of virtuous living is happiness. Our faith lets us take on the messages of the Beatitudes with the hope that any suffering has a good end.

The Theological Virtue of Faith allows us to "believe well" as we seek to understand this mystery. In his encyclical, *Fides et Ratio* (Faith and Reason), Pope John Paul II guides us to understand how people believe. The Pope points out that all people believe in something, even if they are not religious. Aristotle claimed that "all humans desire to know." St. Augustine takes the point further, saying he never met people who wanted to be deceived. In other words, people seek truth. By our human nature, the answers we find will guide our lives.

So, we are built to believe. We want to know our destiny. How do we find the answers? First, we must trust God, or the possibility of God, to give us the gift of faith. Jesus and his followers, the likes of St. Paul, promise that the gift of faith is there for us. It is delivered as "grace." We have that guarantee.

Finally, as we seek to see God through our science window, we are not alone. Many resources beyond this book provide witness and perspectives to help build our faith. It is important to look through this window and share with others what we see. As new scientific discoveries about our

Universe and existence come to us, listen to what others talk about when they describe what they are seeing. Think about what is discovered within a faith community.

Understanding the wonder of God, or the wonder of Creation, should not be a lonely path. When it comes to putting all we find together into a template for our lives, we do not have to figure it all out ourselves. Exploring faith and truth together is one of the biggest reasons to belong to a faith community. We can build off the thinking of generations before us. Just as science has built a massive reservoir of knowledge about our Universe, faith traditions build an ever-growing understanding of our relationship with God.

For most of us, faith does not come like a lightning bolt arriving with immediate force. Faith builds based on the witness and lives of others fed by the grace of God. As faith builds, we act aligned with the values of that community. Faith becomes a habit nurtured by repeated acts for good. Those good habits become virtues within us. We arrive at a point where, even though we cannot prove with scientific means that God exists, the wonders we see through our science window help us to trust, to know, and to believe.

ABOUT THE AUTHOR

Jim Krupka is an author, clergyman, charity director, business executive, husband and father. He has published:

> *The Benevolent Edge*, Westbow Press, 2019.
> *Make Your Marriage Unbreakable*, Westbow Press, 2020.
> *A Fond Aloha,* Maryknoll Magazine, Spring 2021.
> *Praying the Gospel Through the Rosary*, Westbow Press, 2022.

He holds a Master of Arts Theology Degree from Saint Meinrad Seminary. He has over 25 years of service as an ordained Catholic Deacon. Jim currently serves the Diocese of Gaylord, Michigan, and the Diocese of Honolulu, Hawaii.

Over the years, he has served in short-term assignments, such as assisting Catholic Relief Services as a strategy advisor. He was invited to address the United States Council of Catholic Bishops (USCCB) on the Morality of the Global Economy. He served as President of a network of health clinics dedicated to providing healthcare to the uninsured or underinsured. He served as an officer, director, and general campaign chairman for various United Way entities. He co-founded a local charity focused on using music to mitigate bullying in schools.

Deacon Jim has been a leader in business and industry for nearly fifty years. He worked for 30 years in the energy industry. He held numerous executive and management positions, including Director of Strategy for Amoco Production Company worldwide. After early retirement from BP, he served as CEO of a leading winery/chateau company, Chateau Chantal, for 10 years, where he currently serves as Chairman of the Board.

He and his wife of 50 years have five grown children and operate a farm in Northern Michigan.

ENDNOTES

1   New American Bible (NAB). footnote to Gen 6:5-8, 22.
2   Introduction to the Book of Genesis, NAB.
3   Gen 1:6-7, NAB.
4   Gen 1:8, NAB.
5   Notes to graphic, Gen. 1, NAB.
6   Doug Linder, "Bishop James Ussher Sets the Date for Creation," 2004. http://law2.umkc.edu/faculty/projects/ftrials/scopes/ussher.html. Last accessed March 26, 2024.
7   Ibid.
8   Bodie Hodge, "How Old is the Earth?" May 30, 2007.. https://answersingenesis.org/age-of-the-earth/how-old-is-the-earth/, Last accessed March 26, 2024.
9   "Ptolemy's World Map," in World History Commons, https://worldhistorycommons.org/ptolemys-world-map-0. Last accessed March 28, 2024.
10 John H. Lienhard, University of Houston, "Engines of Ingenuity," No. 1568. https://www.uh.edu/engines/epi1568.htm. Last accessed March 26, 2024.
11 Wikipedia. https://en.wikipedia.org/wiki/Age_of_Earth. Last accessed March 26, 2024.
12 Ibid.
13 Ibid.
14 Stephen Hawking, *A Brief History of Time*. (London, England: Bantam Books. 1989).
15 Ibid.
16 Villanova University, "St. Augustine and Cosmology." https://www1.villanova.edu/villanova/artsci/anthro/Previous_Lectures/sustain/AugustineCosmology0.html. Last accessed March 28, 2024.
17 Stephen Hawking and Leonard Mlodinow, "Why God Did Not Create the Universe," *Wall Street Journal*. September 3, 2010.
18 Ibid.
19 Hawking Stephen and Leonard Mlodinow. *The Grand Design*. (New York: Bantam Books, 2010).

20   Institute of Physics, "The big bang." https://www.iop.org/explore-physics/big-ideas-physics/big-bang#gref. Last accessed March 26, 2024.

21   Carlo Rovelli, Simon Carnell and Erica, Segre. *Seven Brief Lessons On Physics*. (New York, New York, Riverhead Books). 2016.

22   Elizabeth Howell and Andrew May. "What is the Big Bang Theory?" *Space.com*. last updated July 26, 2023. https://www.space.com/25126-big-bang-theory.html. Last accessed August 31, 2023.

23   Karlo Broussard, "Catholicism Has No Teaching on the Earth's Age," *Catholic Answers*, Q&A. https://www.catholic.com/qa/catholicism-has-no-teaching-on-the-earths-age. Last accessed March 26, 2024.

24   Rubens, Breughel &. "Garden of Eden." *World History Encyclopedia..* Last modified January 11, 2018. Permission for use: Wikipedia content that has been reviewed, edited, and republished. Original image by Breughel & Rubens. Uploaded by Mark Cartwright, published on 11 January 2018. The copyright holder has published this content under the following license: Public Domain. This item is in the public domain, and can be used, copied, and modified without any restrictions.

25   Pope John Paul II, "Meaning of Man's Original Solitude," General Audience in St. Peter's Square, October 10, 1979. Often referred to as "Theology of the Body" (TOB).

26   TOB.

27   National Gallery of Art. Jean Duvet. "The Marriage of Adam and Eve," probably 1540/1555. Washington, D.C. Right to use: "The National Gallery of Art implemented an open access policy for digital images of works of art that the National Gallery believes to be in the public domain. Images of these works are available free of charge for any use, commercial or non-commercial, under Creative Commons Zero. https://www.nga.gov/notices/open-access-policy.html. Last accessed April 1, 2024.

28   Kerry Lotzof, National History Museum, Hertfordshire, U.K. *"Charles Darwin: History's most famous biologist."* https://www.nhm.ac.uk/discover/charles-darwin-most-famous-biologist.html. Last accessed April 1, 2024.

29   Darwin Correspondence Project, https://www.darwinproject.ac.uk/commentary/religion/what-did-darwin-believe. Last accessed April 2,2024.

30   Ibid.

31   University of Cambridge, https://www.darwinproject.ac.uk/commentary/religion/what-did-darwin-believe. Last accessed March 28, 2024.

32   Colin Shultz, "The Pope Would Like You to Accept Evolution and the Big Bang," *Smithsonian Magazine*, October 28, 2014. https://www.smithsonianmag.com/smart-news/pope-would-you-accept-evolution-and-big-bang-180953166/. Last accessed March 28, 2024.

33   https://www.oldest.org/culture/artifacts/. Last accessed April 1, 2024.

34 Ibid.

35 Wikimedia Commons. https://commons.wikimedia.org/wiki/Commons:Reusing_content_outside_Wikimedia. Last accessed April 1, 2024.

36 Madison Park, "How humans have changed in height in the last 100 years," *CNN Health*. https://www.cnn.com/2016/07/26/health/human-height-changes-century/index.html. Last accessed April 1, 2024.

37 Kenneth Kemp, University of Notre Dame "A Very Short Introduction to the History of Catholic Evolutionism," *Church Life Journal*, May 3, 2021. https://churchlifejournal.nd.edu/articles/a-very-short-introduction-to-catholic-evolutionism/. Last accessed March 28, 2024.

38 Ibid.

39 Richard Klien, "The Human Career: Human Biological and Cultural Origins," (University of Chicago Press, Second Edition, 1999).

40 Bryan Windle, "The Three Oldest Biblical Texts," *Bible Archeological Report*, February 6, 2019. https://biblearchaeologyreport.com/2019/02/06/the-three-oldest-biblical-texts/. Last accessed March 28, 2024.

41 Hawking. *The Grand Design*.

42 Hawking, *The Grand Design*.

43 Carlo Rovelli, Simon Carnell and Erica, Segre. *Seven Brief Lessons On Physics*. (New York, New York, Riverhead Books, 2016). p31.

44 UCSB Scienceline. http://scienceline.ucsb.edu/getkey.php?key=6003. Last accessed March 30, 2024.

45 Ibid.

46 Amy Tikkanen, "Tsar Bomba Soviet thermonuclear bomb," *Britannica*. https://www.britannica.com/topic/Tsar-Bomba. Last accessed March 31, 2024.

47 Email conversation: Treder to Krupka, April 6, 2024.

48 Center for Sustainable Systems, University of Michigan. 2022. "Nuclear Energy Factsheet." Pub. No. CSS11-15.

49 "Nuclear Fission and Fusion." Diffen.com. Diffen LLC, n.d. Web. 7 April 2024. https://www.diffen.com/difference/Nuclear_Fission_vs_Nuclear_Fusion. Last accessed April 2, 2024.

50 EUROfusion. https://euro-fusion.org/fusion/fusion-conditions/. Last accessed April 1, 2024.

51 Pew research, "Global Christianity – A Report on the Size and Distribution of the World's Christian Population." December 19, 2011. https://www.pewresearch.org/religion/2011/12/19/global-christianity-exec/. Last accessed April 4, 2024.

52 Christopher Baird, "Science Questions with Surprising Answers." Blog. January 20, 2016. https://www.wtamu.edu/~cbaird/sq/2016/01/20/where-is-the-edge-of-the-universe/. Last accessed April 7, 2024.

53 Tatem Lenberg, "28 Billion Light-Years Away: The Most Distant Star Ever Discovered," *Discovery*. https://www.discovery.com/space/furthest-star. March 31, 2022. Last accessed April 7, 2024.

54 Ibid.

55 The light we see took 12.9 billion light years to reach us. From its estimated current location, light would take 28 billion light years to reach Earth as the star continues to move farther from Earth.

56 NASA Science. "MARS 2020 MISSION PERSEVERANCE ROVER." https://mars.nasa.gov/mars2020/timeline/cruise/. Last accessed April 7, 2024.

57 National Aeronautics and Space Administration Goddard Space Flight Center. "Imagine the Universe." https://imagine.gsfc.nasa.gov/features/cosmic/nearest_star_info.html. Last accessed April 7, 2024.

58 https://www.gps.gov/systems/gps/space/. Last accessed April 13, 2024.

59 Vickie Stein, "Einstein's Theory of Special Relativity," Last updated February 1, 2022, American Physical Society. *Physics Central*. https://www.space.com/36273-theory-special-relativity.html. Last accessed April 7, 2024.

60 Angelo Stagnaro, "What Is God Really Like? An Exploration of God's Attributes," *National Catholic Register*. Blogs, July 30, 2022, https://www.ncregister.com/blog/exploration-of-god-s-attributes. Last accessed April 7, 2024.

61 Marc Bennetts, "Soviet Space Propaganda Was Atheistic — But Putin's Cosmonauts Fear God," *Business Insider*. July 24, 2014. https://www.businessinsider.com/strange-connection-between-russian-astronauts-and-god-2014-7. Last accessed April 7, 2024.

62 Some id as Gherman Titov. "There is No God!" is a 1975 atheist propaganda poster by Vladimir Menshikov.

63 C. Haub. "How many people have ever lived on earth?" *National Library of Medicine*. February *23, 1995*. https://www.ncbi.nlm.nih.gov/ Last accessed April 7, 2024.

64 John Paul II, Wednesday General Audience, 21st July 1999.

65 Catholic World Mission, "Miracles and the Catholic Tradition." https://catholicworldmission.org/miracles-and-catholic-tradition/. Last accessed April 1, 2024.

66 Ibid.

67 Michael Guillen, PhD. *Believing Is Seeing: A Physicist Explains How Science Shattered His Atheism and Revealed the Necessity of Faith.*. Tyndale Refresh (September 21, 2021). pg 33-34.

68 Glenairn Museum, "ANCIENT EGYPTIAN CREATION MYTHS: FROM WATERY CHAOS TO COSMIC EGG." *Glencairn Museum News*, Bryn Athyn, PA, Number 5, July 13, 2021. https://www.glencairnmuseum.org/newsletter/2021/7/13/ancient-egyptian-creation-myths-from-watery-chaos-to-cosmic-egg. Last accessed April 2, 2024.

69   Wikipedia.   https://en.wikipedia.org/wiki/Ancient_Egyptian_creation_myths#:~:text=The%20earliest%20god%2C%20Ra%20and,Isis%2C%20Set%2C%20and%20Nephthys. Last accessed April 2, 2024.

70   https://www.thebiblicaltimeline.org/wp-content/uploads/2018/10/Joseph-in-Egypt.pdf. Last accessed April 13, 2024.

71   The Bible Journey. https://www.thebiblejourney.org/biblejourney2/48-the-jewish-world-of-the-old-testament/pharoahs-of-the-old-testament/. Last accessed April 10, 2024.

72   Ibid.

73   The Shaka Guide, "The Kumulipo: Ancient Hawaiian Creation Legend," June 01, 2021. https://www.shakaguide.com/article/oahu/hawaiian-creation-story. Last accessed April 2, 2024.

74   Wikipedia. https://en.wikipedia.org/wiki/Hawaiian_religion. Last accessed April 2, 2024.

75   Wikipedia Public Domain. Jean-Pierre Norblin de La Gourdaine (after Louis Choris), Temple du Roi dans la baie Tiritatéa (c. 1816, published 1822) https://commons.wikimedia.org/w/index.php?curid=17263258. Last accessed April 2, 2024.

76   Queen Liliuokalani, of Hawaii, Patron of the Polynesian Historical Society. https://www.sacred-texts.com/pac/lku/lku01.htm. Last accessed April 2, 2024.

77   Francis A. Sullivan, *The Church We Believe In: One, Holy, Catholic and Apostolic* (New York: Paulist Press, 1988). Pg 155-116.

78   AQUINAS'S FIVE PROOFS FOR THE EXISTENCE OF GOD St. Mary's Press. https://open.library.okstate.edu/introphilosophy/chapter/aquinass-five-proofs-for-the-existence-of-god/. Last accessed April 2, 2024.

79   Brett Molina, "Stephen Hawking wrote 'there is no God' in his final book. It's not the first time he's shared that belief," *USA TODAY* October 17, 2018. https://www.usatoday.com/story/news/nation-now/2018/10/17/stephen-hawking-his-beliefs-god-and-heaven/1668456002/. Last accessed April 2, 2024.

80   Catherine Giodano. "Why Stephen Hawking Said There Is No God," Updated November 2, 2023. https://owlcation.com/humanities/Stephen-Hawking-Says-There-Is-No-God-Heres-Why. Last Accessed April 2, 2024.

81   Ibid.

82   Ibid.

83   Christopher Warren. *I've Seen the End of You: A Neurosurgeon's Look at Faith, Doubt, and the Things We Think We Know.* (The Crown Publishing Group, 2020).

84   Warren, *I've Seen the End of You.* p 24.

85   Ibid.

86   https://theweek.com/articles/647050/mother-teresa-sometimes-didnt-believe-god-that-makes-example-faith. Last accessed April 10, 2024.

87 Mother Teresa (Author), Brian Kolodiejchuk (Editor). "Mother Teresa: Come Be My Light: The Private Writings of the Saint of Calcutta," (Doubleday, New York). October 13, 2009.

88 https://en.wikipedia.org/wiki/Blaise_Pascal. Last accessed April 14, 2024.

89 Stanford Encyclopedia of Philosophy, "Pascal's Wager." First published May 2, 1998; substantive revision Sep 11, 2022. https://plato.stanford.edu/entries/pascal-wager/ Last accessed April 2, 2024.

90 Ariel R. Rey, "Global Poll: Most Believe in God, Afterlife," *Christian Post Reporter,* April 26, 2011. https://www.christianpost.com/news/global-poll-most-believe-in-god-afterlife.html Last accessed April 2, 2024.